Discovering *Kes*

A Personal Quest for the Classic 1969 Film

By

Dr. David Glynne Fox

To Neville
Best Wishes
David Glynne Fox

All correspondence for
Discovering *Kes*
should be addressed to:

Irregular Special Press
Endeavour House
170 Woodland Road
Sawston
Cambridge
CB22 3DX

*****

Overall copyright © 2024 Baker Street Studios Limited
Text copyright remains with the author
All rights reserved
Typesetting is in Times font

ISBN: 978-1-901091-91-5

Front Cover: Watercolour of the famous Billy Casper 'V' sign, by renowned
Hoyland artist Richard Kitson. (Courtesy of Richard Kitson and Ronnie Steele).

Back Cover & Page 4: The author with his male golden eagle, Star
(Courtesy of Alex Hyde).

Maps: Courtesy of OpenStreetMap.org.

*****

*****

Every effort has been made to ensure accuracy, but the publishers do not hold
themselves responsible for any consequences that may arise from errors or
omissions. Whilst the contents are believed to be correct at the time of going to
press, changes may have occurred since that time or will occur during the
currency of this publication.

This work is dedicated to the late author, Barry Hines, the cast, and crew of *Kes* and to the many thousands of *Kes* fans worldwide

About The Author

David Glynne Fox was born in Carlton, Nottingham in 1948 and has been a lifelong naturalist and has practised falconry since his early teens. Having written many natural history and falconry related articles for several magazines, he is also the author of three published books. His first, *Garden of Eagles – The Life and Times of a Falconer,* was published in 1984. His second, *Eagle Falconry – A Personal Perspective*, was published in 2012 and his third, *Artist Falconers – The Falconry and Raptor Art of David Morrison Reid-Henry and Ron David Digby*, was published in 2017. He lectures widely on many wildlife subjects, using images from his own extensive collection of wildlife photographs and was for a few years, a visiting lecturer for the MSc degree in Biological Imaging and Photography at Nottingham University. He is a wildlife photographer with many years of experience, particularly concerning macro, or close-up photography of insects and wildflowers etc. He is a passionate historian of the Anglo-Zulu War of 1879, for which he has a doctorate, and also the Alamo of 1836: the Plains Indians of North America, and the Highland Clans of Scotland.

He is also a co-opted member as eagle specialist on the United Kingdom Hawk Board and a past Chairman of the Midlands region of the British Falconers' Club and a consultant for the British Archives of Falconry. He was also responsible for forming The East Midlands Hawking Club in 1968 and the current British Falconers' Club Eagle Group. He has trained and flown many different species of birds of prey, including kestrels and herewith lies his fascination for anything to do with the film *Kes*, and the book from which it was derived, *A Kestrel for a Knave*. David still lives in Nottingham with his wife Gill and has two married children, Joanne and David, and for the last sixteen years, has been flying a male Golden Eagle named Star.

Contents

Introduction

In March 1970, a truly remarkable film went on general release in the U.K. It was remarkable because for once, it featured the story of ordinary working-class people, a rare commodity, which highlighted the mundane life of one imaginary South Yorkshire schoolboy named Billy Casper. Ordinary people the world over, could identify themselves with this film for it basically told their own life stories and for that reason alone, the film has remained not only a classic, but without doubt, one of the best loved films of all time. Hundreds of thousands of ordinary people loved it then, and as I have subsequently discovered, still love it today. Along with countless other people, this film struck a chord deep within me, to the extent that for many years, I desired to write something in praise of this remarkable story. Whenever I watched the film, I could almost see myself up there on the screen as Billy Casper, even down to the point where I kept hawks and was a practising falconer whilst still at school, which was not the lot of so many other *Kes* fans, and it was this fact that rendered the film extra special for me personally. It was so true to my life, as it was to untold thousands of others who had lived through the post war years of the nineteen fifties and sixties. It was a film that made massive cinematic history on the world stage. The film that I am alluding to, was of course, *Kes*. *Kes* is a film that continues to enthral audiences for over half a century after it was produced, and quite rightly so.

This book is an account of my deep personal interest concerning this iconic 1968 film, which was ultimately responsible for turning me into a location detective. In fact, it is the conclusion of over two years of intensive research to elucidate as many facts as possible concerning this important and extremely popular, true to life film. I have based it primarily, although not exclusively, around the original film locations which I have personally visited and photographed over this two-year period, in company with my son, also named David. I have also based it upon certain aspects concerning the author, Barry Hines to help perpetuate his memory, because without Barry, there would have been no *Kes*. Additionally, it has been a real pleasure to visit '*Kes* Country' in the South Yorkshire districts of Barnsley, Sheffield, Doncaster and Hoyland Common and to view, not just the locations first hand, but also to discover and photograph many other *Kes* related memorabilia and associated documents. It has been a real adventure and I have learned so much over the past two years and met many lovely, like-minded people. A few people that I attempted to contact, who could have helped my quest considerably, never bothered to reply, rendering my research that much more difficult and time-consuming, but to my everlasting joy, two or three did, and I shall be ever grateful for their much-valued input. I hope that this book will encourage like-minded individuals to make their own explorations of these locations, and in so doing, will discover, just as I did, as to how *Kes* was created from the use of so many varied sites.

The year was 1968. I remember it well for two reasons. First, it was in April of that year that I first met my future wife, Gill. Second, during the summer months after meeting meeting

Gill, another momentous event was about to occur in the small mining village of Hoyland Common and the nearby town of Barnsley in South Yorkshire, and I remember this particularly well because I may, or perhaps may not, have been involved personally with the making of *Kes*, for I was asked to fly a Kestrel at Hoyland Common that same summer. So how did all this come about and what did it mean for me personally?

In 1968, a local schoolteacher and author, residing in Hoyland Common, Barry Hines, had penned a manuscript that he had titled *A Kestrel for a Knave*. This manuscript, published by Michael Joseph in the same year, became an immediate best seller. The book concerned the basic social life of a working-class Barnsley schoolboy named Billy Casper who experienced a poor, but typical working-class existence at both home and school. He was a street urchin and a misfit in both roles, who eventually finds solace in a kestrel that he takes from a nest in a local derelict building and his life henceforth takes on a new meaning and relieves him somewhat from boredom at school and the dreaded thought of working down one of the local coalmines, as was the lot of so many working-class schoolboys prior to the wholesale closing of the South Yorkshire coalfields during the 1980s. The latter all but destroyed the lives and communities of so many miners during this painful time. This book was so well received that a film producer, Tony Garnett, who knew Barry personally, had asked Barry to send the manuscript to him, and Tony in turn, showed it to the well-known film director Ken Loach. They both decided there and then that it must be made into a film, and the rest, as they say, is history.

The book was highly acclaimed and for many years was used on the curriculum for many schools in the United Kingdom. It is therefore very unfortunate that this volume was dropped from most of our schools due to the actions of a certain senior Conservative member of Parliament, who at the time was the Minister for Education. The book was somewhat critical of the education system, which was true enough, especially concerning the 11-plus examination and its divisive elements, but at the time, was designed to sort 'the wheat from the chaff'. The sad result became the lot of countless secondary modern children of the day, in order that these so-called no-hopers could be filtered out of the system, whilst the 'more intelligent' pupils became earmarked for the more prestigious grammar schools and thus, probably brighter futures. This of course did not go down too well nationally, for it spawned an early class system for juveniles. This system was becoming increasingly unpopular during the late nineteen sixties, because it was so divisive for children of such a young age. This criticism was no doubt the prime reason for subsequently axing *A Kestrel for a Knave* from most mainstream schools by the minister, the education department apparently disapproving of the criticism it had highlighted and which of course was due to their own government failings. I have discovered that *Kes* is still not only incredibly popular today, but sadly is still somewhat relevant regarding schoolchildren and because of this, I firmly believe it should be reinstated in our schools, not least because much of the story is unfortunately still applicable today and of course, it is such an excellent piece of modern literature. It is my hope that this book will encourage younger generations to rediscover *Kes* and the masterpiece that it was derived from, *A Kestrel for a Knave*. So, what was it that was so important for me that it should send me on this lengthy quest for this classic film?

Well, *Kes* reflected my school life so accurately that it almost seemed like it was a rendition of much of my own life and I could easily identify with it, which has not been the lot of most other films of my acquaintance, and, last but certainly not least, it was based on real life events concerning ordinary working-class South Yorkshire folk, which were elements that I had seldom, if ever, witnessed elsewhere, other than in real life. These facts alone were more than sufficient to guarantee for me a total life-long obsession with this feature film.

Because of the reasonable proximity of the *Kes* locations to my hometown of Nottingham, which is barely sixty miles from Barnsley, plus the fact that I may have been involved in the early stages of the film shoot in 1968, *Kes* had resonated deeply within me, probably even more so than for most other *Kes* fans, who undoubtedly identify with the story, simply because I too, as aforementioned, was a practising falconer whilst still at school, which was not true of most other *Kes* fans when the film was finally released in 1970, and this latter fact was just one reason that later gave me the desire to write this rather personal perspective of the film. So, again, why bother to write a book about a film that, by 2023, had been made fifty-five years previously? Surely, it must be old hat by now. I have been asked this question a few times and my answer has always initially been the same, simply because it seemed that the film was about me personally, with two notable exceptions; unlike Billy Casper, I came from a loving family, and I was no petty thief, otherwise, all the rest is reminiscent of my early life, and that, surely is enough. It is a cracking story. However, when I finally decided to pen this missive, I did so with the hope and intention that I could illustrate it profusely with as many images as possible, including stills from the film itself, if copyright permission for these could be obtained. Three excellent books regarding *Kes*, which I will mention later, are very low in images, mostly monochrome stills from the film itself. Images were very important to me for this work and that is precisely why I photographed and visited as many of the sites that I could discover. A picture tells a thousand words and all that. Sadly, copyright infringement reasons have prevented me from using many images that would have fitted well with this narrative, but despite contacting the owners of such, very few ever bothered to even reply. So, as a direct result, I made an early decision to use images largely taken either by myself or my son David and this of course, entailed a lot of travel and research. To those few that have allowed me to use certain images, I am eternally grateful, especially so to Margaret Hines, Barry's first wife who, through the good offices of author and *Kes* enthusiast, Ronnie Steele, gave me full permission to use an image that was essential to this book. I had long desired to use a photograph depicting both Barry Hines, the author, and David Dai Bradley, the star of the film for this work, and this image not only contained both but also, they were holding two of the original three kestrels that were used in the film. For me personally, this was the most important image in the book, for it highlighted to perfection, the main star and author of the film **[1, 2 & 3]**.

My infatuation, as I see it, is no different from other hordes of film buffs seeking some sort of fulfilment by visiting locations and other aspects of their own favourite films, and as for me personally, regarding *Kes*, there are several other reasons as to why I wished to pursue the film further. Firstly, like so many people of my generation, and as aforementioned, it mirrored our lives on many fronts, particularly school days and for me, it highlighted my personal interest in natural history and falconry. Nobody else at my school ever held any interest or knowledge of falconry whatsoever, and very few in natural history come to that, which, just like Billy Casper, the loner Barnsley schoolboy featured in *Kes*, rendered me similarly as something of a loner too. Only two or three of my classmates were ever aware that I kept, trained and flew hawks, so was instead frequently referred to as the weird kid who plays with spiders etc. Because of its removal from the school curriculum, I would imagine that many of the very young current generation have never even heard of either the book *A Kestrel for a Knave*, or the film *Kes* that resulted from it, but their parents certainly will have, for they largely remember it as one of the most popular films ever made. It has been criticised by some for its sad ending, but even so, it remains very popular with most fans. The book itself has enjoyed many reprints since 1968 and has been printed in many different languages and the resulting film, as I have subsequently discovered, was even more popular. Almost everybody that I speak to tells me that it is their favourite film once I mention it and it is still shown regularly on television today. *Kes* indeed also has fans amongst numerous famous people of stage and screen, and in fact, from all walks of life. This knowledge of its popularity was another reason which spurred me on to eventually write this book.

When one considers that even today, many working-class schoolchildren never get a real chance in life and are downtrodden and treated as second or even third-rate citizens from the start, as was Billy Casper, then it seems to me that the book and film are just as relevant today as they ever were. This is one of the main messages in this important work, for it reveals that we still very much have a class society in Britain today, with the gulf between the haves and the have not's increasingly widening. *Kes* is not a film about falconry as such, even though a strong falconry theme runs throughout, but it rather exemplifies the stark existence of the working-classes. The latter are still treated as inferior beings by the super wealthy and so-called authoritarian upper classes, or elite, just as they always have been, but unlike in Billy Casper's, and in my day too, the coalmines and factories that once accepted these 'inferior school failures' in droves, are no longer available to provide mass employment. Additionally, the common workforce has always been paid a pittance whilst their employers have made fortunes from their toil. For most of their lives, many employers have treated their workforce with arrogance, superiority, and at times, downright rudeness, just because they feel that they are above their employees in station and class, and they are fully aware that their workforce dare not answer back for fear of losing their employment. True, without employers, where would the working-class be to provide jobs for the masses? Even so, when one considers the vast fortunes accrued by some employers, it has always been a bone of contention that fairer wages would have greatly helped most of those in need, but few employers recognised this fact, due to their own sheer unadulterated greed.

For decades, out of every generation, around two thirds of our children have been placed on the scrapheap due an examination known as the 11-plus. Fail that, and few children had little chance of bettering themselves with decent future careers, and thus they became a victim of low social standing and division from the age of eleven. Where for example, would famous and very wealthy so-called superior beings be without the working-class to produce their products, buy their records or pay to view their films? Nowhere, that's for sure. Yet many, if not most of these so-called elites would readily snub these underdogs and not give them the time of day. Because somebody possesses great wealth, it does not necessarily follow that they are a better person, they simply have more money, nothing more, nothing less, and this, in my view, does not give them the right to abuse others of lower status. Once one failed the 11-plus, there was literally no possibility of a worthwhile career at the end of our secondary modern school years, and as such, we all left school as no-hopers. I guess it was also a case of as to why secondary modern schoolteachers would then bother wasting their time trying to educate such failures. Therefore, we had no choice other than to leave school with no qualifications whatsoever and could not compete for decent careers with grammar school leavers who had passed the 11-plus and held all the necessary further qualifications. I never realised back then that our teachers in secondary-modern schools would have much preferred to teach the 'more intelligent' grammar school kids and vented their disapproval in various ways upon us. It took the film *Kes* to highlight this aspect for me, for I certainly failed to grasp the enormity of it whilst still at primary school. In fact, long after I left school, I saw the film before I read the book and this situation was even more apparent in the book. The author, Barry Hines, was without a shadow of a doubt, very much against the secondary-modern school system, even though he passed his 11-plus and went to a grammar school. His brother, Richard, was not so well blessed, for he, like me, failed his 11-plus and went to a secondary-modern school, a move which later undoubtedly helped Barry with *A Kestrel for a Knave*, because some of the school tales that Richard related to him eventually found their way into *A Kestrel for a Knave*, albeit with a few modifications. Barry was angry about other matters too. For example, he was angry about the unfair distribution of wealth; he particularly held a disdain for those with inherited wealth, whereby such recipients never even earned it; he was distinctly not a fan of overprivileged people, some of whom probably never did a day's hard work in their entire life. He was against the exploitation of the working class and the destruction of the mining community. In short, he had a lot to be angry about, and who could blame him? He wasn't wrong. It enrages me also. Some of these themes appear in *Kes*.

For these reasons and others, *Kes* is still an important work on so many levels. Some have ventured, could it be re-made today? I personally very much doubt it because in the first instance, there is no way that it could be improved upon. So why bother? In fact, I personally think it would be almost impossible to remake it today, at least, not along the same scripted lines, for to begin with, the world has moved on. The landscape has changed. People's lives have changed, almost everything has changed, sometimes beyond recognition, but the rich/poor divide is still prevalent and increasing. Physical punishment of pupils has long been a thing of the past, but it is shown graphically in *Kes*. We observe the head teacher caning several pupils in succession, which would cause an outrage today because teachers are not allowed to lay a finger on their charges and instant dismissal would follow if they did so. I too occasionally found myself on the wrong end of the cane for it was common practice for misdemeanours when I was at school, so perhaps remaking this aspect would prove somewhat disagreeable to say the least.

Perhaps an even more important reason as to why it could not be remade today could be put down to acquiring the kestrel itself in the first place. Back in 1968, birds of prey in the British Isles were still often classed as vermin by some and shot on sight, and this, despite the 1954 Protection of Birds Act. Even worse, was the widespread use of agricultural pesticides such as organochlorines, which were so far-reaching and soon found their way into the organs of predators, such as kestrels at the top of the food chain. The accumulated ingestion of these harmful chemicals through consumption of their prey, slowly but surely poisoned them and even caused eggshell thinning. This in turn resulted in easily broken eggs which then failed to hatch, thus causing a steep decline in their numbers. Back then, most raptors were becoming nationally scarce because of these and other reasons. I remember as a boy, the place where I lived at Mapperley in Nottinghamshire was surrounded by open fields and woodlands, good kestrel country one would think, but I cannot recollect ever seeing a wild kestrel there because they were already in such sharp decline. Today, the situation is very different, but kestrels have still not returned here because all those same fields and woodlands are now beneath bricks, concrete, and tarmac, so-called urban development, and as such, a victim of 'progress'. This former wonderful habitat has now completely disappeared, rendering the area totally unsuitable for kestrels, and for most other forms of wildlife too. I personally believe that ever constant housing development is an even bigger and more immediate risk to the natural environment than global warming. At least, in the short term. The building of houses and suchlike on green belt land destroys what was once prime former wildlife habitat, whereby any wildlife present is bulldozed to oblivion, never to return. Government ministers seldom, if ever, have any interest in wildlife whatsoever, so this subject is always placed below the bottom rung of the political ladder. Conservation costs money, it doesn't make money, which is reason enough for ministers to avoid the issue. The use of the most harmful pesticides has fortunately been reluctantly banned, thus allowing the raptors to remarkably recover. It is indeed amazing, despite all these threats, that they have managed to survive at all, let alone recover and yet despite all this, kestrels and most other birds of prey have indeed recovered remarkably well. For example, there are more Peregrine falcons *(Falco peregrinus)* around today than since records first began, which is incredible when one considers that in England, we have virtually no real wilderness left at all. Most so-called countryside is basically agricultural farmland, consisting largely of sterile monocultures stretching as far as the eye can see and thus, due to constant ploughing and spraying etc., is subject to much disturbance from normal farming practices. Additionally, we are far more conservation minded today than we have ever been, or at least, many of us appear to be, so to remake *Kes* on this front would be extremely problematic at best. The film apparently caused some conservation bodies to create a furore when *Kes* was first released because it was claimed that it encouraged hordes of young boys who wished to become budding Billy Casper's to raid kestrel nests all over the country. Imagine the response if a remake was to be produced today! The outrage would probably be tenfold. I personally knew many of the falconers residing in Britain at the time the film was made and hardly any of us ever heard of anyone taking kestrels illegally, because of the film or otherwise. I am not saying that none were taken, because no doubt some were, and for some, it was probably the beginning of their falconry careers, but they were taken in nothing like the numbers that some have claimed, because not only would we most likely have heard of such, but more importantly, because of the pure fact that kestrels were in such a steep decline back then and so seldom seen that it would have rendered the taking of such large numbers of young hawks, virtually impossible. It appeared to me that these allegations were used primarily as conservation propaganda, largely against falconry itself, which some deem archaic. This is a shame, because if the truth was widely known, which it usually isn't, falconers have been directly involved in initiating most of the world's raptor conservation projects, often through captive breeding programmes and suchlike and so their expertise is almost always sought, but seldom acknowledged. Even so, if the film was to be remade today, I wonder how the taking of the kestrel could be satisfactorily and realistically portrayed? Falconers nowadays breed all their own birds and have done so for decades, so the need to remove them from the wild has been totally unnecessary in Britain for many years. To remake *Kes*, instead of climbing the walls of a ruined building or tall tree, the star of the film, Billy Casper, would simply have to visit a breeder and purchase one, which would hardly have the same appeal on screen now would it? It would also be a major diversion from the original film script and screenplay. Yes, a home bred kestrel could easily be placed into a suitable cleft in a ruined building or a hole in a tree and then a new young Billy filmed climbing up to 'take it', but I feel this would still have the same disastrous effect of showing the bird being taken 'from the wild', thus resulting in the undesirable aspect of inspiring more youngsters of today's generation to go out and take their own kestrel from the wild. This would be a disaster, not least because falconers and falconry would be blamed, when, in fact, kestrels are of little or no use for falconry purposes. Because of their small size, they are difficult to train, especially regarding weight management, which can be rather tricky at best, especially for beginners and they can live for many years, a consideration that few young boys would be likely to take into consideration. Get the weight aspect wrong and the bird will either die through malnutrition or fly away due to being overweight. The bird protection laws today are much stricter than previously, and conservation attitudes have changed markedly. But I must ask the question, would young boys today be aware of the law, and would it make much difference to them by putting them off from taking a kestrel from the wild? Probably not. All British raptor species today must be accompanied by an article 10 certificate which legally covers individual birds, together with the name of the breeder and the closed ring numbers on the bird's legs also being legally documented etc. This demonstrates 'proof' of captive breeding and in many cases, if there are any doubts about the validity of origin, DNA samples will prove legal parentage, or not. None of this applied in 1968 when *Kes* was made, except that a licence was still required to take one from the wild. For this reason, I have added a postscript detailing some of the inherent difficulties experienced in training birds of prey, hoping that this will act as a deterrent for would-be young falconers. I would be aghast if I thought that this book would result in the illegal taking of any wild bird of prey.

Today, there is absolutely no need to take kestrels, or any other raptors from the wild, because as formerly stated, they are so easily acquired from experienced breeders, so why risk prosecution and a heavy fine, or even worse, risk a serious, or even fatal fall from a building or tree when most species of birds of prey are readily available from many breeders up and down the country? Showing all this on a remake of *Kes* would make little sense and would, as aforementioned, deviate greatly from the original script and render it much less interesting. Additionally, for the benefit of beginners, over the last few years much more information on falconry is freely available, much more so than it was in 1968, when I was self-taught from a couple of books. Since then, many excellent and up to date falconry treatises have since been published. Also, several regional clubs have been formed to help newcomers, rendering information on the training of birds of prey and their availability far more accessible for beginners and several falconry centres have sprung up nationwide where useful information may be obtained. So, from this perspective at least, *Kes* could not really be remade today along the same lines. So, the original film will no doubt remain the great classic that it is for all time. I sincerely hope so.

As aforementioned, even back in 1968, it was illegal to take birds of prey from the wild without the appropriate licence and the three used for the filming of *Kes* were all taken legally under a specifically issued Home Office licence and after filming was completed, all three were hacked back to the wild, none the worse for their moment of fame. I feel it is very important to emphasise this fact. So, to recap, acquiring kestrels for a remake of *Kes*, would not be a problem, and neither would be selecting an experienced falconer to train them, provided of course that this element was duly shown on film. Today, there are many excellent and experienced falconers in the United Kingdom, all of whom would be up to the task. Having trained many raptors over the years, I could do it myself. However, I still feel that a remake along these lines would likely still instigate the problem regarding the illegal taking of kestrels from the wild, so from this aspect alone, the making of another *Kes* film would be problematic and probably undesirable at best. Additionally, we no longer have secondary modern schools in the United Kingdom, so scenes such as the caning of pupils would also have to be scrapped, rendering a very different film altogether. So no, I don't believe that *Kes* could be remade along the same lines as the original format.

Therefore, many years later, once I became aware that many of the original film locations could still be located, I was desirous of recording in camera, as many of these sites as possible for posterity, plus anything else related to the film that I could locate that may even have only slight connections to *Kes*. The following is the result of the author's research and travels to '*Kes* Country'.

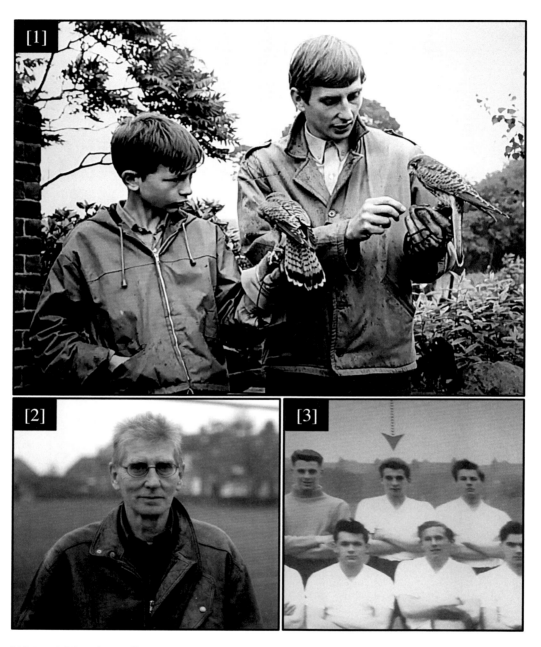

[1] David 'Dai' Bradley, as Billy Casper, and Barry Hines, author of *A Kestrel for a Knave*. (Margaret Hines collection). [2] Barry Hines in later life. [3] Photograph of the England under 19's football team with Barry Hines arrowed. (Margaret Hines & Ronnie Steele collection).

Ken Loach Exclusive Interview

[Ken Loach (left) and the author (right) with the *Kes* film poster centre stage]

Although I had completed writing about my personal quest for the classic 1968 film, *Kes*, I had never met a single member of the cast, or crew. Ken Loach, as director, was most certainly someone I had longed to meet. At the time of writing Ken is in his mid-eighties, and I knew that he was still very busy directing films (though he has said that his 2023 film *The Old Oak* is his last), so the possibility of an interview seemed somewhat remote at best. However, upon contacting his office and outlining the contents of my book Ken granted me (and my publisher Dr. Antony Richards) just such an interview. This was beyond my wildest dreams, especially after unsuccessfully trying to contact others who were involved in the making of *Kes*. It was agreed that a 30 minute slot would be made available commencing at noon on Valentine's Day 2024.

On the appointed day, I needed to go to an address on Wardour Street, in the City of Westminster, and find an unobtrusive grey painted door, which I found quickly enough and then a thought struck me. I had seen this building before. My mind flashed back to the BBC documentary called *Looking for Kes,* presented by Greg Davies. Greg had visited these very premises during his encounter with Ken Loach. I remembered viewing the BT Tower in the background and seeing Greg press the intercom button on the door to alert

Ken's attention. I did the same and made my way up a few flights of stairs to a small conference room on the second floor, the walls of which were adorned with framed posters featuring many of Ken Loach's films. A few seconds later, we were joined by the great film director himself. After shaking hands, we sat around the same table that Greg Davies had sat whilst interviewing Ken about *Kes* and in the background was the same large, framed poster of Billy Casper in the goalmouth on the famous football pitch.

It was time to get down to business and this is where our preparation came to the fore since between myself and Antony, we had composed thirteen questions which broadened the scope beyond just *Kes* to include much more of Ken's film making, and even touched on his politics. In view of the latter, it was made clear to Ken that if he was not comfortable with any question that we would simply move on to the next. Politics is a risky and divisive game which can easily get out of hand, but fortunately, nothing of the sort occurred. Ken was everything I had read about him. He was modest, softly spoken, and a true gentleman. I liked him immediately. Antony read out the carefully prepared questions in turn, allowing for Ken to furnish us with answers in his own time which he did faultlessly. I learned a lot. Such is the mark of the man that not only were we given full and candid answers to each and every question, but that he stayed with us until he needed to leave for another appointment at one o'clock and thus he had allowed us double the time we had been originally granted.

The following is a (lightly edited) transcript of that interview which we hope the reader will find as interesting to read now as we did when listening to Ken Loach, the director of twenty-eight films over a fifty-six year period.

Question 1 – Politics and Career Choice

I would like to start with Ken Loach the man and what might be the most contentious question which media people might say is 'the elephant in the room'. Throughout your life you have been said to be a very political film maker. From my view having seen your work I would say that is rather unfair ... I don't think that your films are that political per se.

I think that you make films that highlight a social problem, and I think that what you want to do is to tell a story, and at the end when people have watched that film you want them to go away and think about that problem, and better still if they then want to do something about that problem to make the world a better place ... then excellent, but that is not overtly political in itself? With Kes *it was the problems of poverty/working class struggles (a common theme in your work) but in particular education, a hopeless landscape/future (employment) and how one ordinary boy/not necessarily a hero finds sanity/something to live for/something to care for in Kes.*

But your own background was a grammar school and then Oxford (St. Peter's College) to read law ... a very different world to that of Billy Casper, so I wonder what made you go down the career path you did? Not a natural choice since with your background it might be expected that you would be making something rather glossy such as Brideshead Revisited *with the Oxford connection, or with your law background* Rumpole of the Bailey *in collaboration with John Mortimer!*

There are several pointers wrapped up in this aren't there? As regards political you have to define politics. In our group which joined together during the 1960s with Roger Smith, Tony Garnett, Ken Trodd and Roy Battersby among others, in the group of us within the *Wednesday Play* where we all got together. The politics was defined by the struggles of the '60s, we joined the Labour Party and we worked for Harold Wilson in the '64 election to support him and realised quite quickly that that wasn't going to change the world and at the same time, a new politics was developing, a new left and summarised mainly in one of its slogans which was 'neither Washington nor Moscow', in other words, to imagine a reconstruction of society based on socialist principles which both wanted fundamental changes from capitalism in the west, Washington, and rejected the Stalinist interpretation of Moscow.

The political discussion underpinned everything that we did, we read the books, the great socialist classics and the struggle to defend the gains of the 1917 Revolution, what that meant, and the long history of Labour and the struggle defining the trade unions and re-evaluating the 17th century English revolution, a bourgeois revolution to install freedom for the many, instead it was about power for the few. That is the context – what goes on in Parliament is too narrow for the definition of politics.

Politics determines everything about our lives, how we live together, the societies that we construct, and the relationships we have to work and what is produced. Our income and its security determine our choices. Politics determines how we live together. With that as a definition, as filmmakers, we tell stories about people that the audience can engage with and would want to meet, but which also shine a light right into the heart of conflicts inherent in our society. The implication of the story reveals a political position, if you think about it, so when it comes to *Kes*, the choices Billy Casper has, he is either semi-skilled, or unskilled labour, that's the future that society has set out for him, because that's the need that they have, they are not about personal fulfilment.

You know there is also the rhetoric about fulfilling everyone's potential, it is not about that at all. They want a certain amount of unskilled and a certain amount of semi-skilled labour. Billy Casper is at the lower end of under achievement in school so that is his destiny. We've seen another side of him which is commitment, talent, care, empathy, a long-term capacity to concentrate, which is something he could never do at school and his social circumstances have made it very difficult for him to develop into a good scholar, but potentially, he has so much more, but society is not interested. Why is society not interested? Because it is not built on human need, it is based on the economic requirements of that society. So fundamentally it is very political, and Barry Hines was deeply political. He wrote another book called *The Gamekeeper* and there is an introduction to him which John Berger wrote a piece about and which he sent to Barry. Barry wrote back and said, 'Thank you, finally, someone has realised that this is a deeply political book, because it is about an ex-steel worker who becomes a gamekeeper for the local Lord of the Manor'. A lot of the reviewers didn't get that at all, for it was a contradiction, moving from an exploited worker to someone who is defending the rights of property against his fellow workers. Barry was deeply political, but it shouldn't strike you as being a political lecture, although the core idea is deeply political.

Question 2 – The Initial Inspiration for *Kes*

When you were going to make Kes *I assume that you started with the book. Whilst reading* A Kestrel for a Knave, *were there any specific sections which made you decide that the film just had to be made? Also were there any scenes that just had to be included in the film? The 'money shot' as directors might say!*

I never call it the 'money shot'… that's an unpleasant term and I would never use it. I have just been talking to somebody who's writing a book, and he keeps using the term 'kitchen sink'. I told him never use the word 'kitchen sink', it's a patronising term used by bourgeoisie film critics … a way of demeaning working class life … infuriating[1] … in other words it puts it in a box and says that working class people do not have lives of subtlety and nuance, it's just women in aprons with their hands in the kitchen sink. The real drama in their eyes is the middle class people.

First of all, I read it and loved the book as everyone does. Tony Garnett, who knew Barry introduced me to him. We met him in Hoyland Common, walked across the fields to the woods and everything about Barry was absolutely spot-on, a lovely, funny man of absolute integrity and enjoyment, so we laughed a lot, so there was no question, we knew we would make the film from day one. Then it was a question of going through and finding the essential narrative but also including the football scene. You couldn't cut it because it was so good and it says so much about school and the teachers and Billy himself as well, and it leads into a good section as well about his shorts and the consequences for him being in the mud. It was a question of finding the essential lines and it's a judgement as you go through and work it out really, which I just did with the book and then passed it by Barry and Tony. It was fairly straightforward, for it is all there in the book … it was only an editing job really.

---

[1] At the suggestion that *Kes* was a 'kitchen sink' drama.

Question 3 – The Film Ending

At the end of the film, what made you stop with the death and burial of Kes, instead of pressing on with the ending originally written by Barry Hines. I must confess to be slightly disappointed with your ending for I wanted to know what happened next ... did Billy Casper go and get revenge on his brother, did he accept the situation, or something else? As Kes runs to only 1 hour 51 minutes there was certainly time to add a few minutes to the film without making it seem overly long.

I think it just felt like the end of the story, just simple, that's the end of *Kes* and also, I don't like films that go beyond an hour and three quarters. You have to have a really good reason to go beyond one hour forty-five, or one hour fifty minutes.

Is it that it would have included too man flashbacks and been difficult to film really?

Yes. It just seemed the wrong choice. Billy buries *Kes* and walks away. That's it.

I think also that your ending made people think afterwards of the different scenarios that might happen next, and also made people to want to read the book ... and so actually looking at it from that perspective you did it perfectly.

Question 4 – On Using Non-Professional Actors

In Kes *I know that you used non-professional actors for a lot of the parts, and I assume that wasn't just to save on expense, but that you wanted to add authenticity to the film. However, did you have any major concerns using ordinary people, especially the schoolchildren ... after all it has been said never direct with children or animals, and you used both in* Kes *so were there any problems, especially with reference to the schoolchildren?*

No, it is the other way round, if you find the right people. We tried people over and over again and did little improvisations to see who could do it. Some could do it up to a point and others did it really well. I mean, teachers knew how to be teachers and a lot of it is kids in classes, Colin Welland had been a teacher, the other teachers are from the school itself, the headmaster was from another school nearby and Barry had been a teacher. Brian Glover who played the games master, taught English at a nearby school but was also a professional wrestler in the evening. He understood everything about the part and had a great sense of humour, and went on to become a very successful actor. And David Bradley, was just one of the thirty kids at the right age at the school but was the perfect Billy Casper. Extraordinarily talented and the nicest man you'll ever meet. What luck we had!

A test of a good script is always if people have a real connection to the part that they are playing, will the words fit? Well Barry's words fitted entirely, so we shot it in sequence as always.

They would have their scenes a day or two beforehand and they would have all the time needed to really absorb it although we would never say learn it word by word, so it's really just read it, know it and we'll play the scene. We never rehearsed, but because Barry's writing is so good, because it just fitted and because they weren't trying to remember every dot and comma, what you are after is the impulse that comes from them. They own it, it is theirs and it just comes out and they knew it, so 95% of the time it was Barry's words although sometimes it was in their own words, but the essence is Barry, because what you need to film is not a rehearsed speech, it's a genuine interaction between people on screen and is the truth of the moment and that matters more than anything. If the moment is false, the speech may be perfect but it is of no value because there is no truth in it. When Billy Casper is in the schoolroom, describing the process of training the bird, he did it three or four times, never got it perfect, well, there is no such thing as perfection, because they are all a bit different, so it's essentially what Barry wrote, but the interaction with the kids, it was David's struggle to articulate and that is point of the scene. It's not telling the audience how to train a kestrel, it's about a boy who has never spoken in class before but can hold the class.

Because Mr. Farthing is a good teacher, he allows him to do that and you see the lad's talent, the talent is revealed in his struggle to articulate. So, I didn't want him to learn it word for word because then he wouldn't struggle. The struggle is what is important, and because he trained the bird himself, he knew what he was saying. He didn't know in advance he would have to speak about it, he just knew it because he had done it and he had learned the names. It is trying to create a situation in which you set it up so that the people who are in it are able to experience it rather than just rehearse.

Question 5 – On Selecting the Filming Locations

We've considered the actors so now to the locations. For most films I guess you use a location scout who chooses the main location and then the lesser ones are selected nearby to save on costs. For Kes *were you involved yourself in choosing the locations, or did you use a location scout or company? When did you know that you had the right location, or did some locations just present themselves once you had started filming?*

No, we went to Barry, we just worked through him. We went to the school. It was very easy. We said to Barry just show us where everything is. He showed us and those were the locations used.

Question 6 – On the Use of Monochrome Film

I believe that you originally wanted to film Kes *in monochrome, and I assume that was to give the shots an austere backdrop? Then later you decided to use washed out tones. Was this to convey the idea of working class people and their struggles?*

I've always loved monochrome films and prefer black and white still photographs because the images are stronger. It's just a preference, but the danger was that it would look dated in the cinema, so we went for colour, but the other problem is that colour can be very distracting, so we always tried to find subdued colours, mainly slightly drained in intensity. A lot of design work goes on so you don't have bright colours, like a bright red in the corner of the screen which distracts and takes your eye away from what you really want an audience to look at. So, a lot of design work goes on which is actually hidden, so that the audience is unaware that their attention is being guided to the image on the screen which you want people to look at and not to be distracted by irrelevant colours. The grading is important. It was not a question of the colours being washed out, but we were careful that the contrast should not be too high, because that makes the colours more intense. They should seem real, but harmonious and as I said, not distracting.

Question 7 – Challenges and Conflicts and the Role of a Director

When you were filming Kes *were there any conflicts or difficulties, either creative or personal, and if so can you tell us about them and how were they resolved?*

No, not that I remember. Part of the job of directing a film particularly, and of the whole team is that it has got to be a pleasing experience for the people in the film. That then brings out the best in the actors, the production crew and everybody else … then people have confidence. What you need from people in the film is vulnerability and they will only allow themselves to be vulnerable if they are absolutely secure and amongst friends and that everyone is respectful of them.

So that's part of the trade and certainly for the people in the film. They've got to sense that it is a very happy place, because again they have never been involved in doing a film before and the moment that they feel there's a tension, they are going to ask, what's this and close up.

Mistakes will always happen and if something does happen, you have to smile about it and make a joke of it, and if you cock it up, you say it doesn't matter, it's only a bit of film through a camera, and so we have a cup of tea and do it again. It's not a problem and so long as you can stick to that, you get the best out of people, which is the point of the job.

The first rule of directing is good manners. Nobody says that at film school but that is it, rule number one is good manners. And rule number two is to resolve all potential difficulties before you begin – for example each department has to be sure that it has good working conditions and can do its job with support from every other department. If problems do arise, they need to know that production will resolve issues in an understanding and supportive way to their satisfaction. And rule number three – is there has to be some shared laughter – even when you are filming the most serious scenes!

Question 8 – The *Kes* Trailer

So you have finished the film and it goes off to the distributer and the marketing people. When the 3 minute trailer[2] voiced by Patrick Allen was shown in cinemas the emphasis wasn't on Kes *itself, but on loneliness and being different, and it highlighted that Billy Casper was no hero. The tag line they used in that trailer was 'You might think it's funny ... You might think he gets what's coming to him ... You might be wrong'. There was nothing about his background, social problems, or education so I wonder whether you were disappointed with the marketing and the bias it took?*

I don't remember the trailer to be honest. I simply had nothing to do with it. I think the distributers didn't know what to do with it at all. When United Artists first saw it, they said they understood Hungarian better. They had no idea. They premiered it in Doncaster, which was bizarre and Roy Mason, who was the right-wing M.P. for Barnsley, with whom we had little in common, either politically or in any other way came and Tony, me and Barry ended up having a political disagreement with him. He seemed to be there under pressure and had little interest in the film. It was due to the support of two good critics, Derek Malcolm in *The Guardian* and Nina Hibbin in the *Morning Star*, both of them promoted it and I think largely because of their input, the film came to the old cinema in Oxford Street, a famous cinema, The Academy where Marks and Spencer now stands.

Question 9 – The Reaction to *Kes*

Did you have any preconceived ideas as to how successful Kes *was going to be while you were making it? Did it shape your career as a director and make it easier to get other projects off the ground?*

No, it was very little noticed at the time, it just gradually established itself. It wasn't in the big cinemas, it didn't have a long run.

---

[2] The original film trailer can be viewed at https://www.youtube.com/watch?v=BGcllKvfnYs.

I have a figure here that says that it only grossed $62,423[3] which I don't suppose is a lot in cinema terms.

No, it wasn't expected to go abroad. The one that established us in Europe was *Family Life* which followed it and which didn't take enough as they said to pay for the usherettes, but *Kes* really began very slowly, and it has just gradually taken off and established itself, but it took a long time, and because no-one had any confidence in us.

The thing is that it is such a cracking story and a reason why I have written the book as I wanted to bring it back to the current generation as most of them have never heard of it which I think is a shame as it is such a great story. It should go back on the school curriculum as modern day literature in my opinion.

Barry's writing is very fine and most certainly worth it. It's not for me to say about the film, but the book itself is a wonderful book, and I cannot imagine any other author catching the rhythms and the comedy of South Yorkshire better than Barry. He just gets it absolutely. He has a wonderful ear, and a great eye for character and the nuances of daily life.

Question 10 – On Film Awards and Funding

Despite what you say Kes *did have some success at the time. In 1971 you were nominated for various BAFTAs for* Kes. *You missed out on Best Director, but that is no great shame as so did David Lean and Robert Altman who were fellow nominees[4], but Colin Welland won Best Supporting Actor over Bernard Cribbins in* The Railway Children, *and David Bradley got Most Promising Newcomer to Leading Film Roles over somebody called Liza Minnelli ... I don't know what happened to her career! So you did have considerable success with* Kes, *and I would say that at the time a film like yours was never going to be seen as mainstream as if you look at the Oscars that year the world seemed to be in love with war films such as* Patton *with 7 Oscars,* Tora! Tora! Tora!, M*A*S*H *and* Cromwell *so I don't think that the world was quite ready for Kes.*

Yes, I have never been interested in the States and I don't care for American commercial cinema. We've never raised money in America, we've always raised it in Europe. We've always looked across the Channel, not the Atlantic and so in a way the work we've done, and *Kes* is an example, it owes a lot to the European tradition of film making, particularly to the Czech cinema and very little to the Americans.

---

[3] Figure quoted on the IMDB.
[4] The winner was George Roy Hill for *Butch Cassidy and the Sundance Kid.*

You are certainly appreciated in Europe and have won many awards at the Cannes Film Festival.

Financially, we lean on Europe, more than here, although not in *Kes*, for *Kes* was entirely funded by United Artists, because of Tony Richardson who enabled it to happen. It had already been turned down and we may have had to delay it a year. I owe a great debt to Tony Richardson because he was our link, and because he had made the successful *Tom Jones* it was on his word that United Artists trusted him and so they paid for *Kes*. I think it cost about £160,000 pounds or £170,000 pounds.

Question 11 – On a Changing Society

How do you think that society has changed over the last 50 years since you made Kes *– has it got better, worse, remained the same or just different? For example, are there still the same social problems with education, and do you think that* Kes *made a difference in highlighting those problems?*

I think from the point of view of the Billy Casper's of this world, everything is far worse. Billy could look forward to not the job he wanted, but he had a job. It would be a secure income. He could raise a family on the income and the health service was not a home for profiteers. There would be a house and the society seemed sustainable because we were still in the wake of the post war wealth settlement, which was the establishment of a partial welfare state, so that was in place for Billy Casper mid-1960s.

Come the 1980s and the attack on the organised working class by Thatcher to reduce the power of labour, the cost of labour, to re-establish profit for British capital, that was an onslaught on the unions, culminating in the miner's strike obviously, and that was a decisive battle that opened the door to the whole neoliberal project, where capitalism is unfettered by social restraint or inhibited by having to protect worker's rights, so that has been worn away and that has meant that workers don't have the same rights. There was mass unemployment, so for now, Billy Casper would be faced with casual employment. There would be a whole alienation of people from their communities, and the political process. Poverty has led to drug problems, so Billy Casper would inevitably have taken drugs, whether he would become fully addicted, or whether it would just be part of his scene, who knows?

I think the arrival of the digital world and social media brings all those consequences that nobody knows about. Social media itself can be vindictive and cruel, so would he have the hours to even consider training a hawk, because he would be on his phone all the time. He wouldn't have the space for his imagination to fly, so in every respect, socially, economically and from the point of view of his choices and the care the state takes of young people, everything is worse. His health provision is worse, because when

Nye Bevan's health service functioned, it wasn't about private health companies ripping off the health service.

Barry saw the fault in the education system but at least it didn't have the problems that the education system has today, brought about by the problems the kids have, and the problems families have, and the effects of poverty.

Homelessness is much worse now. Probably his mother would have had a whole situation with having a house, so in every social aspect, because the demands of capital are not about caring for people they are about profit. Everything is worse. The housing situation is far worse. I mean there was council housing then, but Thatcher destroyed that and the Labour Party itself has moved so far to the right. It is a march to the right; it is not even a drift. There is no chance of re-establishing the principles of the health service under the current Labour regime. Welcome the profiteers. The N.H.S. is on its way to becoming simply a logo, not throughout of course. A lot of people are doing their best, and are brilliant when you get to them, but how do you get to them?

Question 12 – Would *Kes* Ever Be Made Today?

I know that you are officially in retirement now, but if somebody today persuaded you to make Kes *for the first time, or a remake of it, how different would it be in style and focus do you think?*

I don't think you could make it now for the reasons I've said. The culture has changed … it couldn't be made today.

Question 13 – The Ken Loach Legacy

Summarising in your very long career you have made 28 films over a 56 year period between 1967 and 2023, some apparently needing subtitles in the States. You started in the theatre initially going on to countless television works with some never broadcast as being thought of as too political. You've been very successful with personal awards for Riff-Raff, Hidden Agenda, Raining Stones, Land and Freedom, The Wind that Shakes the Barley, *and* I, Daniel Blake … *but when inevitably Clive Myrie or Sophie Rayworth or whoever it is when that sad day comes on the B.B.C. News announces that 'Today we are very sorry to report the passing of film director Ken Loach' what are they going to say next? I think that they are only going to mention two of your earliest productions …* Cathy Come Home *and* Kes … *and they will then associate you with those three words you hate, 'kitchen sink dramas'. Would that be a fair legacy? How would you like to be remembered?*

How broadcasters would present me is probably not what friends would say, because the writers in news tend to think in clichés, and so whatever cliché they choose is not something I would speculate on really … it is up to them. I think what always matters is, if you are remembered at all, it's what your friends and those who know you think.

You will be remembered for many films I feel. I just hope that you are proud of what you achieved with Kes.

Well it's always us. They never talk about me, they never talk about my film, it's Barry's film, it's Tony Garnett's film, it's David Bradley's film, Chris Menges' film, Brian Glover's film. We are always a team and as they say in football 'there is no 'I' in team' so it's really important that.

Not all directors would say that. Most would say that 'there is a 'me' in team', and it's 'me the director'.

No, it isn't. I think that's propaganda to sell the film. Without a writer you are confronted with a blank piece of paper which is why I always work with a writer. For the last thirty years that's been Paul Laverty, who has been a wonderful friend and comrade as well as being a fine and creative writer. We see the world in the same way, laugh and get angry about the same things, and always find the time to catch up on the football.

It's what the people you know think that counts. If you are political you expect to make enemies. Politics is a serious fight, and if you are serious and attack or argue against the established powers, they don't like it. It's interesting that they never go for the subject matter … they make up things at a personal level and that's how they always attack. They've done it to me … the press is tainted by that, some will go for it straight on, and some will echo the smear like the B.B.C. That's the consequence of taking on the right-wing establishment. It's a consequence you have to live with, but it's the people who know you and what they think and whether you have stuck with the principles that is all you can hope for.

And you have never thought of standing yourself for election?

No, I'm not a politician. I think also people who do what we do whether writers, directors, painters, musicians or whatever, our job is not to justify or suggest little compromises here to make a bigger advance there, our job is to say look these are our principles on which we stand. They are non-negotiable and you cannot betray them and that's a real function, because otherwise the principles get lost in the details of daily political combat. That is certainly the case now, and the need to assert the fundamental principles of a just society has never been greater.

Our time with Ken Loach had come to an end, sadly, but we had almost a full hour in his wonderful company. The time had passed so quickly. We just had time for a quick photo session, where Ken and I stood either side of the large, framed *Kes* poster, and for him to sign one of my copies of *A Kestrel for a Knave.* It had been a day that I would long remember.

As a final comment it is interesting to note that just five days after our interview with Ken Loach at the 2024 BAFTA film awards that although Ken Loach did not win in the category of Outstanding British Film for his final production, *The Old Oak*, that Samantha Morton in her acceptance speech for the BAFTA Fellowship cited Ken Loach and *Kes* as being the original inspiration that made her choose acting as a career. It just proves, if proof were needed, that Ken Loach is an inspiration in himself.

Chapter 1

Kes Comes to Town
& the BBC's *Looking for Kes*

Barry Hines had decided to call his novel *A Kestrel for a Knave*, due to an old list that has found its way into print many times, most notably in falconry treatises, though nobody seems to be one hundred per cent certain that this list is historically correct, from whence it originated or, if it is even accurate. It apparently first appeared in *The Boke of St. Albans,* attributed to Dame Juliana Berners in 1486 and has passed down the centuries ever since and concerns birds of prey as status symbols for the various social hierarchy, whereby one could denote a person's station in life from the hawk that they carried upon his or her fist. It should be remembered that back then, falconry was the 'football' of the day and was extremely popular, even involving royalty. As one would expect, the finest birds were reserved for the higher echelons of society and woe betide any serf who may be discovered with a hawk above his station in life. For the record, I will repeat this list here, although there are other very similar versions.

An Eagle for an Emperor
A Gyrfalcon for a King
A Peregrine for an Earl
A Saker Falcon for a Knight
A Lanner Falcon for a Squire
A Merlin for a Lady
A Hobby for a Young Man
A Goshawk for a Yeoman
A Sparrowhawk for a Priest
A Musket (male Sparrowhawk) for a Holy Water Clerk
A Kestrel for a Knave

Our hero, Billy Casper fits this list adequately enough to be denoted as a knave, reflecting his low social standing and class. Therefore, a kestrel, back in the day, would have been appropriate for his station in life. If the above list holds any truth, it is perhaps a fair demonstration of how times have changed, at least in some aspects, whereby a lowly knave like me, and indeed, Billy Casper himself, is now allowed to fly the emperor's bird, the mighty Golden Eagle *(Aquila chrysaetos)* without fear of prosecution, provided of course, that the bird has been legally acquired in the first place. If anything, the film version was even more successful than the book, although perhaps nobody could have foretold how nobody could have foretold how successful the film would eventually become when Ken Loach and his team arrived in Barnsley and Hoyland Common in South Yorkshire to begin the filming of *Kes*. As aforementioned, the book was published in the same year that the film was produced, in 1968. The story was about a young working-class schoolboy named Billy Casper, who hailed from Barnsley in South Yorkshire and who led a very deprived and in fact, quite miserable existence. He came from a broken home; his father had left due to his mother's promiscuous behaviour, and he also suffered at the hands of a bullying older brother named Jud. His school life was no happier than his home life, but all this improved when he found a nestling, or eyas kestrel in a ruined building close to his home. He now had something of real interest to focus upon which helped him blot out the otherwise drudgery of everyday life. For a while at least. This film version has remained remarkably popular ever since. On the downside, most of today's younger generation have little or no knowledge of either the film or the book, primarily because of its axing from the school curriculum, but for many adults, as I have subsequently discovered, it has remained their favourite film of all time and it was even voted the 7th Best British Film of all Time by the British Film Institute, which is quite an accolade.

When *Kes* was first released, locally in Doncaster, South Yorkshire, it became an instant box-office success, breaking all previous records apparently. This was especially notable as there are relatively few books and films that cover the northern towns, cities, and social life in general, particularly ordinary working-class life. *Saturday Night and Sunday Morning*, by Alan Sillitoe, is one of the few that spring to mind. So, when *Kes* appeared, it was like a breath of fresh air. As previously alluded, it told the story of a 14-year-old schoolboy, Billy Casper (played by David 'Dai' Bradley) who came from a broken home, had an older bullying brother named Jud, (played by Freddie Fletcher) and an uncaring mother, Mrs. Casper (played by Lynne Perrie of *Coronation Street* fame). Because of his mother's rather promiscuous behaviour, with various 'uncles', Billy's father had left home leaving the family to fend for themselves, although this aspect was toned down considerably in the film version. The story was brilliantly written by Barry Hines, a former schoolteacher who was born and lived for much of his life in the mining village of Hoyland Common, just south of Barnsley in South Yorkshire. When Barry wrote the book, it was titled *A Kestrel for a Knave*, a title which he apparently always preferred to the film title, *Kes*, although Barry did choose the name *Kes* for the kestrels used in the film. Yet Barry didn't train kestrels at all, this came about due to Barry's brother, Richard, who had an interest in falconry and who had previously trained and flown kestrels. Barry used Richard's expertise for his forthcoming book. The title for the film Kes itself was chosen by Tony Richardson, a British film legend who managed to persuade United Artists to fund the production.

Yet *Kes* almost never made it to our screens. There were no highly paid big stars; the only professional actor was the late Colin Welland. It was low budget, no sex, little violence, and the wrong kind of bird! National General, a Hollywood company that had previously backed the film, pulled out. Thankfully, United Artists USA stepped in. Even the producer, Tony Garnett, initially had his doubts, for, as he stated after viewing some of the rushes:

"We are going to end up with an X certificate film that's not understood beyond five miles outside of Barnsley."

Tony of course was referring to the strong Barnsley dialect. I can well understand Tony's viewpoint, even though I personally love it. For the record, here are a few typical Barnsley phrases:

Asthagoritwiththee? – Have you got it with you?
Purremineer – Put them in here.
Burraberritiz – But I bet it is.
Arse end a nowhere – We are lost.
Guwin t'shop, does tha wannowt? – I am going to the shop; do you want anything?
Gerrit tha sen – Get it yourself.

The above examples are just a few of many delightful Barnsley phrases. But is this so different from many other English regional dialects, such as those from Birmingham and the West Midlands, Cornwall, and County Durham, all of which have strong dialects? I don't believe it is. However, because of the Barnsley dialect, *Kes* was apparently shown in America with subtitles or dubbing. Because of this and other setbacks, not least from film critics, it still took two years for the film to be generally released and when it finally made it, *Kes* premiered not in London, as would be the norm, but at the ABC cinema in Doncaster, South Yorkshire in March 1970.

The producer, Tony Garnett, who knew Barry personally, was blown away by the story and immediately showed the manuscript to director Ken Loach, who too was very enthusiastic. Both realised that the book was crying out to be made into a film and this film centres around what is basically a single day or two in Billy Casper's dreary and mundane existence, although from acquiring Kes to training her to fly free would have taken him three or four weeks at least, if not longer, as he had no previous falconry experience. This timeframe was telescoped in the film and gave the impression to the uninitiated that Kes was trained, more or less, in a single day, which of course was not possible.

However, once the film was released, it began breaking all previous box office records for many cinemas throughout Britain. It was one of the very few films about working class people that have ever been produced and it was widely received. It highlighted the often-humdrum life of the ordinary person in the street and was critical of the school system back then, where all who failed the 11-plus examination were reduced to a lifetime of dreary, mind-numbing, low paid manual labour, factory work or a dangerous life down the coal mines. It demonstrated that youngsters back then didn't just fail the 11-plus, they became a victim of it, and it decided the fate of around two thirds of each generation. This failing was very much on the mind of the author, Barry Hines, when he wrote *A Kestrel for a Knave*. It showed that we still have a class system in this country and that the gap between the wealthy and poorer people is ever widening. This scenario was the outlook for Billy Casper, the main star of the film, played brilliantly by David 'Dai' Bradley, who was a 14-year-old schoolboy when Ken Loach's film crew descended on St. Helen's Secondary Modern school in Athersley South, near Barnsley in South Yorkshire.

I also went through the same school system, as an 11-plus failure, which was another of the main reasons for writing this book, because I experienced many of the same problems that Billy Casper faced at school. There were also two other reasons. The first one being that I had been a practicing falconer for several years before *A Kestrel for a Knave* was published and *Kes* the film was released, and am still a falconer today, more than six decades later, and it was the falconry scenes in *Kes* that particularly appealed to me [4]. The second reason came about because I flew a kestrel for a film crew in 1968 which I believe could quite possibly have been for *Kes*. This is how it came about:

I had formed the East Midlands Hawking Club early in 1968, and the club soon included members from Nottinghamshire, my home county, Lincolnshire, Leicestershire, Derbyshire, and South Yorkshire [5]. As a direct result, the club was soon asked to give flying demonstrations at various venues within these counties. It was at one such display for a village fete somewhere in South Yorkshire, quite possibly in Holmfirth, *where Last of the Summer Wine*, the longest running comedy series ever, was filmed, that one of our members, Mr. Jack Lee had been approached by a film producer who asked if we would be prepared to fly our kestrels for a film that he was about to produce [6]. Both Jack and I had, amongst other species, a kestrel each, but these were not from the British Isles, although they were of the same species (*Falco tinnunculus*) for the latter was protected by law and could not be taken without an appropriate government licence. Our birds were imported from India, not that we wanted kestrels, we didn't, because they are not considered as true falconry birds, not least because they were naturally mouse and insect feeders, which is not the type of quarry that most falconers would favour. These two, and others, had come over with a consignment of larger falcons that we had imported for various club members, but the supplier did not always have enough of the larger falcons to meet our needs, so the order was often made up with other species, such as kestrels. Unfortunately, this happened quite frequently. In those days, hardly anyone wanted such species, so we were generally stuck with them and tended to use them as display birds. This is precisely why Jack Lee, and I came to be flying kestrels on our flying exhibitions. Once we became more widely known, we were often asked to take part in such country fetes and sometimes the occasional film work.

In fact, I had quite forgotten all about the latter display until about a week later, when Jack called round to my house to enquire if my kestrel, named Eos, was still in flying order [7]. I replied in the affirmative. Jack then told me that he had just received a telephone call from the producer he had met when we gave our demonstration in Yorkshire and had arranged a date for us to visit a village that I had never heard of called

Hoyland Common, near Barnsley in South Yorkshire. I also had a Saker Falcon and a Goshawk at the time and suggested we should also take these with us as they were larger and thus more spectacular, but Jack said no, it had to be kestrels and only kestrels would suffice, nothing else would do, which is no doubt why Jack was approached in the first place. Jack had told me that the producer had approached him whilst I was in the arena putting Eos through his paces and he had apparently been impressed, hence his interest for his film sequence. I still thought it odd because the larger hawks were far more impressive, but the producer was adamant, so only our two kestrels, plus Jack and myself, set off up the M1 motorway for the pre-arranged rendezvous.

We had been given instructions as to where we needed to meet the producer, and this turned out to be in a pub car park, which I think was on Hoyland Road, Hoyland Common, a few miles south of Barnsley [8]. I am reasonably certain that the pub was called The Star, but as we often did this sort of thing, I didn't really take that much notice of the surroundings, so I could well be wrong, after all it was a long time ago. Either way, we pulled into the pub car park and was met by the producer (at least I presumed he was the producer) and a cameraman. There was no sound engineer as no sound was required and no other individuals that might make up a film crew were present. We were informed that we personally would not be in shot as only flying sequences of the kestrels were required. Fair enough we said, and with that we followed the two men in our car until we came to a large open field. To this day, I am uncertain as to the exact location of the actual field we used, but I remember that it was not far from the pub, and I think it was beside the Sheffield Road opposite the end of Hoyland Road. I only came to this conclusion many years later after making several visits to Barnsley and Hoyland Common to secure the images required for this book, and this field seemed very familiar, but again, I could be wrong.

After the camera had been set up, it was decided that I would fly Eos first, so I wandered into the field and cast him off into the wind. He flew well before I let him have the lure after a few minutes. The producer seemed delighted and so it was then Jack's turn to fly his female kestrel, which also performed equally well. Whilst Jack was flying his bird, I wandered over to the producer to ask him why we were doing this? I had presumed it was for a documentary about wildlife and I was concerned about the presence of jesses (the leather straps that are fitted around a hawk's legs in an ingenious time-honoured fashion so that the hawk can be handled with ease,) but that these were trailing behind the birds in flight and obviously would appear as trained birds and not wild ones, but he said no, not to worry about that as it was for a feature film about a Barnsley schoolboy who trains a kestrel, so jesses would be present anyway. That statement reassured me considerably. A few minutes after Jack had completed his flying sequence, we both walked out into the field again and flew both kestrels together as a cast. This completed our session.

On our way back to the parked cars, the producer told us that these were basically insurance shots, just in case the young kestrel's taken under licence for his film did not perform well enough for some reason or other. The producer thanked us for our trouble, and we parted company, with us heading southwards for Nottingham. We heard no more about this episode, ever, so we never really knew if any of our sequence was ever considered for use in *Kes* or not, the latter of which is entirely possible and I for one, promptly forgot all about it. Of course, it has to be said, and I emphasise the fact that the flying sequences that Jack and I did that day could just as easily have been for another film entirely and not *Kes* at all, and I guess I will never know for certain, but if not, it was surely quite a coincidence, for it was at the same time, the summer of 1968, the same venue, Hoyland Common, near Barnsley in South Yorkshire, and, according to 'our' producer, was about a Barnsley schoolboy who trains a kestrel, which exactly mirrors *Kes*, does it not? Whether or not our input at Hoyland Common was for *Kes*, I have ever since, rightly, or wrongly, felt some sort of personal affiliation with *Kes*, which is precisely another one of the main catalysts as to why I have written this volume. I have never heard of another similar film being made at that time, or since for that matter, so it is anyone's guess as to whether our flying sequences had ever been intended for inclusion in this classic masterpiece. Personally, I cannot think what else our inclusion could have been for, but I will leave it to you, the reader, to judge for yourself. I often wonder what became of the film footage that we shot in Hoyland Common. Did it end up on the cutting room floor and subsequently the bin, or was it preserved, who knows? And that is where everything rested for more than fifty years, or at least, as far as I was concerned. I didn't even view the film until the mid 1970s and despite scrutinising the footage, I didn't recognise any of the flying sequences, or the background field that Jack Lee and I were involved with, and this is quite understandable, because the three kestrels that Barry Hines's brother Richard trained for *Kes* behaved almost impeccably, so ultimately there was no need for our 'insurance' shots, if indeed, that is what they were.

By some strange coincidence, two years later, I was back in Hoyland Common in 1970, to purchase a large Finnish female Goshawk *(Accipiter gentilis)* named Rudi, from a falconer named Terry Hibberd. Of all the places in Britain whereby I could have obtained Rudi, Hoyland Common had reared its head yet again. It seemed weird that I returned to a place that until our former filming sequences, I had never heard of before. It was almost as though it was calling me back purposely. As I had heard nothing about our filming session there, it seemed pointless mentioning it to Terry, but unbeknown to me, the film was about to be generally released and titled *Kes*, at around the same time as this, my second visit to Hoyland in 1970.

Over the intervening years, I often viewed *Kes*, for it was shown regularly on television and I later purchased a copy of it on DVD. I first saw *Kes* on the big screen at the Elite cinema on Parliament Street in Nottingham city centre around the mid-1970s, but never since have I seen it on such a large cinema screen. Initially, Ken Loach, the director, wanted to produce the film in monochrome, but the American backers insisted it be filmed in colour. Here is where the genius of cinematographer Chris Menges came to the fore. The film was pre-flashed to desaturate the colours, using possibly an Arriflex

Varicon, or something similar, and it paid off, for the resulting film footage does indeed give the impression of a stark, washed-out landscape, full of austerity with its diluted tones. Ken also often used non-professional actors to achieve realism, so for *Kes*, he spent a lot of time matching possible actors to match the roles. He basically wanted actors that *were* the characters, rather than merely professional and highly paid actors simply playing the parts. He did an excellent job, and so did the non-professional actors to their everlasting credit. After viewing the film for the first time, I sought out and picked up a first edition hard back copy of *A Kestrel for a Knave*, in a bookshop in Whitby, North Yorkshire and was amazed at how closely the film followed the book. This is most unusual, especially with Hollywood backed movies, so full credit to Ken Loach, the director and Tony Garnett the producer for largely sticking to the 'script' as written in the book. Unusually, there was hardly any need for a screenplay because it was all there within the pages, although one was certainly produced for I have seen and handled Barry Hines's personal copy.

Kes has many thousands of fans worldwide, but few seem to have ever written much about it or produced a book, which, considering the half-century since it was produced, plus its profound popularity, I found quite amazing. I have always expected one or other of the cast members to pen their experiences whilst making this once in a lifetime film opportunity and their part in it, but I am unaware of any of them ever doing so. I understand that David 'Dai' Bradley, around the year 2005 was planning, or even working on such a volume, but I have been unable to discover if it was ever published. Only Simon W. Golding, with his excellent *Life After Kes*, is one of perhaps three individuals who have taken up the baton, although Simon's book, as the title suggests, is concerned mostly about the subsequent lives of the film cast and crew. It is without doubt, the finest complete book concerning *Kes* that has ever been published. However, little has been covered about the actual film locations, upon which my work is largely based. Barry Hines's brother, Richard, gave an excellent account of his role as falconry supervisor on *Kes* in his lovely book *No Way but Gentlenesse - A Memoir of how Kes, my Kestrel, changed my Life.* Both books are indispensable for *Kes* enthusiasts, as is of course, David Forrest's and Sue Vice's *Barry Hines, Kes, Threads and Beyond*, which I am sure will remain for many years the classic book to consult for any future Barry Hines biographer [9]. Apart from these three classics, one would be hard pressed indeed to find another volume concerning this amazing film.

Life After Kes, the book written by Simon W. Golding was a treasure trove of *Kes* facts, especially as it specialised in covering all the cast and crew members involved. Simon was extremely fortunate in meeting virtually all the cast and crew of *Kes*, whereas at the time of writing, I have yet to meet a single one of them. I purchased the first edition of Simon's book from eBay, a signed copy too, published in 2005, although I knew nothing about its publication until sometime during 2021 whilst researching for this, my own book, and it was not until late in 2022 that I discovered that a second edition had also been published in 2016 by Apex Publishing Ltd. I bought a paperback copy and discovered that not only did it have a new foreword by Melanie Sykes, (the first edition had a foreword by Michael Winner) but there was also an additional chapter, which formed chapter 28. It was titled *The First Ever KES Reunion 2005*. I must admit, that as well as the Barry Hines Memorial in Barnsley town centre, and the Barry Hines blue plaque on one of his former homes in Hoyland Common, neither of which I was aware of until I had begun my research, but also, I was totally unaware that a reunion had ever taken place. Oh, how I wish that I had known about these events at the time.

This reunion in 2005 was of great interest to me because many of the surviving cast members were present. What an occasion that must have been for them. The reunion was also the catalyst for the launch of Simon W. Goldings's excellent first edition book. Ironically, it took me over fifteen years after its launch to discover that this remarkable book and the reunion had even existed. The book launch at the National Museum of Photography, Film and Television was to coincide with the 12th Bradford Film Festival in Bradford, just north of Barnsley and Hoyland Common. Tony Earnshaw, the director of the museum helped Simon to put it all together. A screen talk was decided upon, followed by a screening of *Kes* itself. To this day, as aforementioned, I have only once seen *Kes* on the big screen, and this was at the Elite cinema on Parliament Street in Nottingham with my wife Gill in the mid 1970s. Since then, I have only viewed it on television, so the full-size screen viewing must have been a real treat for all those present. Several members of the cast and crew were seated beneath the big screen for the talk, hosted by journalist Anthony Haywood. Sat next to him from left to right was Ken Loach the director, Barry Hines the author, Tony Garnett the producer, Colin Welland who played Mr. Farthing and finally, the author of *Life After Kes*, Simon W. Golding.

Other members of the cast and crew were also present, but some were either away on holiday or had sadly since passed away. One of the latter was Bob Bowes, who played the headmaster Mr. Gryce. He had unfortunately passed away in 1979. Another was Lynne Perrie, who played Billy Casper's mum, and although she was still alive, she was seriously ill and in a coma, and she sadly passed away in 2006. She was cremated at Rotherham crematorium but there is no marker for her final resting place and as such, it would have proven pointless to even attempt to photograph the location. Brian Glover, who played Mr. Sugden, the brilliant PE teacher had also sadly passed away from a brain tumour in 1997 and is buried in Brompton Road Cemetery in London. There is now a blue plaque for Brian Glover erected on Chennell's Bar on Wellington Street in Barnsley, which is where Brian had filmed a documentary in 1976 about his hometown. It is not far from the Alhambra shopping precinct where the Barry Hines Memorial statue is situated. Ken Loach, David 'Dai' Bradley, and Barnsley author Ronnie Steele, amongst others, were all present on this occasion. It was erected in September 2022 and yet again was something that I only found out about afterwards. Ronnie Steele, author of *Build it for Barry*, and member of the Kes Group who instigated the Barry Hines Memorial and the blue plaques, has also written a new book called *A Blue Plaque for Brian Glover*, which features a painting of a scene from the famous football match from *Kes* on the front cover.

But back to the reunion. Freddie Fletcher, who played Billy's bullying brother Jud was away on holiday in France. Had I been Freddie, I think I personally would have flown back for this event, after all, one can go to France at any time, but this event was a spectacular, never to be repeated, one-off. John Cameron, who wrote the evocative musical score for *Kes*, was away in Los Angeles, although his wife kindly took the trouble to represent him. His haunting musical soundtrack for *Kes* is still available on a CD. I have a copy of it in my small *Kes* collection. Over a dozen other cast members made the pilgrimage to Bradford that day. What I wouldn't have given to have just been there? Other cast members included Joey Kaye, whose immortal 'Marrow Song', is still popular today. Bernard Atha (1928-2022), who played the Youth Employment Officer, Eric Bolderson who played the farmer at Tankersley Old Hall (Monastery Farm), Zoe Sunderland, who played the librarian (she actually was a real librarian at Barnsley library), Trevor Hesketh, who not only played Casper's teacher in the film, but was also David Bradley's form teacher in real life, and also some of the school kids from Casper's class, such as Mike Padgett, Jim Ryder, Roy Turner and George Speed were also present, to mention a few. Even four of the five members of the 4D Jones band turned up, one was apparently ill so couldn't attend, he must have missed a spell-binding occasion. This band had played at the Cudworth Hotel during Jud's and Mrs. Casper's night out. The unexpected and crowning glory was the surprise appearance of David 'Dai' Bradley himself. He gave a short speech which was well received by all present.

Apparently, over three hundred members of the public, all no doubt avid *Kes* fans were also present, and it appears that that number could have been doubled or even trebled. I also guess that most of the members of the public who attended were from local regions, for I certainly didn't see any advertisements for the function back in Nottingham. However, admission was by ticket only. I won't go into too much detail, for this can all be found in the second edition of Simon W. Goldings, *Life After Kes*, which is often available from Amazon, eBay, or some good book shops. I sincerely hope that Simon Golding sold many copies of his book, which took a full two years of often difficult research to complete, and I know from personal experience, just how difficult this kind of research can be, enjoyable yes, but difficult and very time consuming.

After my filming experience with Jack Lee, fifty years then passed before a wonderful BBC documentary, called *Looking for Kes*, presented by Greg Davies was shown on BBC 4. Greg visited three or four of the actual film locations, which was a revelation to me, because I thought most of the locations were film sets, such as the chip shop, the betting shop, Tankersley Old Hall, the school etc., all of which I believed would have subsequently been dismantled, as in a great many films. This documentary gave me the idea that I could use the original film locations as the baseline for my own work, showing them as they appeared today and frame it all around these, if of course, I could find them and additionally, if they still existed. So began a two-year quest to find and photograph as many of the film locations as possible. Fortunately, Kes was filmed in a comparatively small area, unlike many other films which have been shot in multiple sites all over the country, or even the world. So, for Kes film buffs, all the locations can be easily visited over a comparatively short space of time. It took the author much longer because he did not have the advantage of this book to guide him.

To commemorate the fiftieth anniversary of the making of *Kes*, the BBC had produced this wonderful documentary *Looking for Kes*. I couldn't believe it. Watching this BBC documentary on one of my favourite films of all time was almost unbelievable. It reignited a flame within me to the extent that I became obsessed with the story all over again. Strangely enough, I never normally read novels and never have done so since leaving school, and although I have many hundreds of books in my personal library, the only novel I possess is *A Kestrel for a Knave*. However, although a novel, much of it is based on real life events and in part, is also based on Barry Hines's brother Richard, who also trained the three kestrels that were taken under Home Office license and were used in the film so, on these points alone, the novel was a welcome addition to my library. It is this true to life aspect of *Kes* that particularly appealed to me and no doubt countless other *Kes* fans too. A book entitled *The Goshawk*, by T. H. White was another work that inspired the Hines brothers. Although very well-written, this latter work is today widely acknowledged in most falconry circles as a treatise of what NOT to do when training a hawk. It was one of the falconry books that had also found its way into my own library during the early years of my falconry career and would have been the same book that Billy Casper referred to when speaking to his teacher, Mr. Farthing about goshawks: "Ave been readin' up about 'em."

Perhaps a short resume of the documentary would be appropriate here.

Looking for Kes opens with an elevated view of presenter Greg Davies, walking in the middle of a road, dragging a wheeled suitcase behind him, on his way to begin his week-long quest. To my surprise, he informs us that *Kes* inspired him whilst still at school, at a time when the book version was almost automatically placed on many school's curriculum. He first visits the director, Ken Loach, in his apartment and interviews him about the making of *Kes*. He also visits the late Tony Garnett, the producer, who sadly passed away in 2020 and who also filled in more details for Greg, such as the fact that there was hardly any need for a screenplay because it was all written within the pages of the manuscript.

Greg then arrives in the village of Hoyland Common, where much of the film was shot and where Barry Hines was born and lived for much of his life. He interviews the northern author Kit De Waal, who reveals to us that there are comparatively few successful working class northern authors, and how she was inspired by the works of Barry Hines. As also was northern author Milly Johnson, who still lives in Barnsley and who was in fits of laughter because Greg had to literally kneel-down to interview her in the Hoyland Common Working Men's Club, due to him being so tall and he was partly obscured by the upper part of the bar, out of camera shot! Greg wanted to interview Milly about her dealings with Barry Hines and as a result, even more mirth was brought to the fore when Milly informed Greg that she had never met Barry Hines! Milly is also a member of the Kes Group.

The Working Men's Club is situated on Fitzwilliam Street and is where Barry Hines frequently visited to have a quiet drink and to observe local people and listen to their stories, several of which eventually found their way as characters in some of his novels. Greg interviews Mick Whitaker, manager of the Hoyland Common Working Men's Club who informs us about Barry's frequent visits to the club and that the latter was very attracted to the ambience of the place, sometimes visiting with his wife or sometimes alone. Fitzwilliam Street itself features in *Kes*, where we see Billy Casper walking up the street after obtaining Kes's meat from the butcher's mobile van, parked near the lower end of the street.

Barry Hines had been married twice, and so Greg visited his first wife Margaret, who informed him that Barry's spelling was not too good, and so they both often sat together correcting his hand-written manuscripts. Barry's first novel was called *The Blinder*. This was about a footballer who, had things turned out the way he wanted, would have been Barry himself, because he was an excellent footballer and had apparently been offered trials for Manchester United. He would have been a George Best with six A levels! Barry also played for Barnsley FC for a time. In a former television interview, Barry informs us that he had previously only ever read comics, such as the *Dandy* and *Beano* and had never read a novel or a book of any type, until he went to Loughborough College in Leicestershire, where he was loaned a copy of George Orwell's *Animal Farm*, (about eighty pages in length and in large print) and it was this that set him on the literary path which was to lead to *The Blinder*, *A Kestrel for a Knave* and several other novels and screenplays.

Greg then visits Barry's second wife, Eleanor Mulvey. Eleanor appeared visibly upset in this piece to camera, for it was filmed not long after Barry's unfortunate demise due to Alzheimer's disease in 2016. I was very moved by this scene. Eleanor also revealed that Barry was really pleased when someone commented appreciatively on his work. It really made his day. I only wish that I personally had had the opportunity to meet this wonderful author and to have shown my own appreciation, but it was not to be, and I never did get to meet him, which was most unfortunate, because he could have helped so much with my research.

Shortly afterwards, we meet the star of the film David 'Dai' Bradley himself. Unfortunately, due to the rules of the actor's union, Equity, David was required to alter his name. There was another, older actor named David Bradley who, amongst other roles, played the caretaker Argus Filch in the wonderful Harry Potter films. The younger actor, therefore, changed his name to 'Dai' Bradley, which apparently appeased Equity. The latter met up with Greg Davies at Tankersley Old Hall, not far from Hoyland Common and from where Freeman, one of the kestrels used in the film was taken from its nest (eyrie) in the crumbling stone walls. Here they are joined by a falconer (un-named

41

unfortunately) who brings his male kestrel along and allows both Greg and David to fly the bird to their gloved fists in the field in front of the ruined hall. They are then joined by Richard Hines himself, Barry's brother, who not only flies the kestrel but also a male (jack) Merlin *(Falco columbarius)*, which is Britain's smallest raptor. Had it not been for Richard training kestrels as a youngster, Barry would probably never have written *A Kestrel for a Knave*, or at least, not in the way that he did, and thus we wouldn't have the film *Kes* today, so *Kes* fans owe Richard a great deal too. As a point of interest, had the book and film not been about a boy and his kestrel and instead, been about a boy and his dog, or his pet cat, I doubt very much whether the book or film would have been produced at all. This is not to decry dogs, or cats in any way, but they don't carry the same awe-inspiring appeal as do raptors. Or, perhaps, as a life-long falconer myself, am I too biased? I was rather surprised that Greg and his film crew didn't visit Barry Hines's grave, which is not far from Tankersley Old Hall, or if they did, the footage didn't make the final cut. At this point in time, I had no concrete idea as to the location of Barry's final resting place.

We then move on to Billy Casper's school, now the Carlton Academy, where Greg talks to present day pupils about *Kes*. This wasn't the school that was used in the film however, the Carlton Academy wasn't even built back in 1968 and is on a different site. I at first thought the real school was at nearby Monk Bretton and was called St. Helen's Secondary Modern. Although I was later to discover that St. Helen's Secondary Modern was not at Monk Bretton at all, but at Athersley South, on Carlton Road, it is St. Helen's Primary school that is situated at Monk Bretton. Apparently, according to the website Kes-BillyCasper.co.uk, run by David 'Dai' Bradley, St. Helen's Secondary Modern was demolished and replaced by the Edward Sheerien School, and this too was apparently demolished in 2011. I later discovered that the St. Helen's Primary School is still intact. This building, as I discovered, appeared in a very similar design to the original secondary school in *Kes*, the latter of which was David 'Dai' Bradley's school in real life and was where much of the filming took place in 1968, although it sadly no longer exists. It has since been replaced by The Holy Trinity School.

Greg then visits Sheffield University and in particular, the Arts Tower, where he meets Professor David Forrest, who was a lecturer in Film Studies and Faculty Director of Learning and Teaching. Professor Forrest then takes Greg over to view artefacts from the Barry Hines Archive which, or so I first thought, were housed in the Arts Tower. As aforementioned, he is also the author, together with Sue Vice, of an excellent and scholarly book called *Barry Hines – Kes, Threads and Beyond*, which was another volume that was soon to be destined for my bookshelves. Anyone wishing to research the life of Barry Hines and his works will find this book indispensable and very thoroughly researched. We are next shown the original first draft of *A Kestrel for a Knave* which is a handwritten manuscript, a real literary Holy Grail if ever there was one and is something that one day, I hoped to see for myself. Barry Hines's woollen college scarf was next to be shown and we are informed that this was knitted for him by an aunt, because purchased ones from shops were too expensive, and as this was being shown to Greg, David Forrest suggested that he sniff it, both stating that the aroma reminded them of their own school days. This important artefact is not allowed to be washed or cleaned in any way. Another artefact shown was Barry's final school report. I am so pleased that Sheffield University is curating these wonderful artefacts for the nation, and this was an obvious place for me to visit at some future point during my research.

The next destination was the fish and chip shop back in Hoyland Common. This is where, in the film, Billy spends some of his bullying brother Jud's hard-earned cash from his job down the local coal mine. Jud left him a note to place the money on two horses, but Billy spends the money instead on fish and chips after a man in the betting shop, in his opinion, tells Billy that the horses stood little chance of winning. Julie Goodyear, the actress who played barmaid Bet Lynch in the long-running television soap, *Coronation Street* can, in the film, just be seen in partial silhouette behind the counter. To my great joy, the fish and chip shop was still there and the current owner, Dave Rose, in appreciation of the film, had changed its name from The Harbour to Casper's Fish and Chips, which I thought was amazing and I made up my mind that I was going to visit this place as soon as possible. In the documentary, the shop is still designated as The Harbour on the main signboard, but all smaller signage referring to this naming had since been replaced entirely with Casper signs. Dave Rose is shown handing Greg and David Bradley their portions of chips. "Bloody good chips too," says David Bradley. More about this later.

In the film, before school, Billy Casper is shown at the newsagents from where he delivers newspapers on an early morning paper round. Billy steals a bar of chocolate whilst in the shop and later 'borrows' a copy of the *Dandy* comic from his bag and is shown reading this in front of a huge, industrial, clanking, noisy coking plant which is billowing clouds of smoke skywards. He reads a section concerning Desperate Dan, a character which I remember well from my own childhood comic-reading days. The coking plant is now long gone and, amazingly, green fields and not buildings now occupy this rural scene. Here we see Greg and David chatting about Kes filming locations, sitting on a barrier by the busy A6195 road. It was no doubt this scene, Tankersley Old Hall and Casper's Fish and Chips shop, that I suddenly realised that these were existing *Kes* film locations which finally sowed the seed for me to visit and photograph these and other *Kes* film location sites, if I could find them, and thus began my own research journey.

Greg also interviews Jarvis Cocker, who is a musician and front man of the band *Pulp*. Jarvis has been a lifelong fan of *Kes*, especially at school where the book was used regularly on the English literature curriculum. He loved the swearing parts when, for once, whilst reading extracts from *A Kestrel for a Knave*, it was okay to swear in school and he took full advantage of it, raising his voice when the word 'bastard' came up in print. The book hadn't even been written when I was at school, so I never had such an opportunity, but my daughter, Joanne did. Strangely though, my son David who is only three years younger than Joanne, never had the opportunity. Was this the beginning of the end of using *A Kestrel for a Knave* in some schools? In fact, Joanne borrowed my paperback copy for her schoolwork, and I never even noticed that it had 'disappeared'. Well, I did have rather a lot of falconry and natural history books! Joanne returned it later in a somewhat more dog-eared state. I still have it. I emailed Jarvis Cocker to ask if he would kindly write a forward for this work, but like most of my requests for information, strangely, no reply was ever forthcoming. I even wrote to David 'Dai' Bradley through his website for the same reason, but nothing ever came of it. I never received a reply.

We are then treated to a piece of comedy. Here we see a clip featuring comedians Vic Reeves as Mr. Farthing (Colin Welland) and Bob Mortimer as Billy Casper (David 'Dai' Bradley). The latter holds aloft a long stiff wire with a model kestrel in flight fixed at its summit. Vic Reeves then approaches and asks Bob Mortimer:

"Does it fly then Casper?"

Bob replies:

"Yes sir, it's flying now sir."

I thought this scene was a very comical send-up of *Kes*. You really must see this clip to appreciate it fully.

Greg is then shown returning home and gives a brief resume of his amazing trip. It is an excellent documentary and well worth watching, especially if you are, like me, an avid *Kes* fan.

Without a shadow of a doubt, *Kes* is still very popular today with thousands of *Kes* fans worldwide. For a great many people, it is still their favourite film. I would also venture that were it no longer popular, as someone once suggested to me, then why would the BBC send a well-known presenter, Greg Davies, and a full television crew to spend a whole week in Barnsley to film this documentary? That must have cost quite a bit, surely? Why also would the Kes Group take the trouble to commission a sculptor, at a cost of £106,000, to create a wonderful memorial to author Barry Hines, in the form of a life-sized kneeling Billy Casper holding Kes, cast in bronze and placed in Barnsley town centre for all to admire? There are other memorials too, which I will come to later. In my opinion, if *Kes* was no longer popular, due to so-called apparent lack of interest, none of the latter would ever have taken place. For me personally, I wholeheartedly believe *Kes* still has hundreds of thousands of fans worldwide, I have even met some of them and discovered that *Kes* also mirrored much of their own lives too, as it did mine on many levels, to the point where no other film has come even close. This is precisely why it will always remain a very important classic.

My quest from 2021 to 2023, to photograph most of the known *Kes* film locations in and around Barnsley in South Yorkshire, demonstrated to me just how much has changed since 1968. There are no coalfields left now, where once their conspicuous winding gears dotted the landscape, all are now long gone. Today there is very little industrialisation, and almost no factories. School-life has also probably changed almost beyond recognition, although by how much and whether for the better is perhaps a matter of conjecture. Certainly, like most secondary modern schoolchildren from the 1950s and

1960s, I saw a lot of myself in much of the book and the film. Like Casper, I remember getting the cane at school a few times, sometimes unfairly, sometimes not and being bullied on occasion too, although I usually gave as good as I got, as did Billy Casper. It wasn't until I viewed the film and later read the book, that I suddenly realised that my secondary school teachers had largely treated us as failures right from the beginning. To them we were all useless 11-plus failures who were never going to be good for anything anyway. I failed my 11-plus deliberately because I wanted to go to a secondary modern school with my primary school friends who had failed the previous year. I didn't know anybody at grammar school and wanted to stay with all my old friends, well, who wouldn't? Certainly, none of our primary school teachers ever appraised us of the 11-plus situation, and how it would harmfully affect our futures if we failed, primarily because I now realise that they too probably didn't care one way or the other either and no doubt in their eyes, we were misfits anyway and besides, the many factories and coalfields required a great deal of manual labour to keep them going, so failures at school were an important national asset. As Billy Casper reiterated:

"Teachers don't care about us, and we don't care about them."

Seldom have truer words been spoken.

For me, *Kes* was not just a film, it was real, and that was most important, from my point of view at least, and as such, it has become a large part of my life.

When I began this quest, I had no intention whatsoever of writing a book on the subject. That aspect never entered my head because I never thought I would ever have anything like enough material to fill a book. My original motivation was to put together an illustrated talk covering as many aspects of the film as possible to add to my long list of wildlife talks that I give to various clubs and societies from time to time around the country. However, during my visits to Barnsley and Hoyland Common, I gained a lot more information and material than I originally expected and as such I thought about possibly writing an article for submission to a specialist falconry magazine. This article shortly reached fifteen thousand words, which was far too long for an article, unless serialised over two or three issues. A book, however, was still not really in the offing until a chance remark made by Dave Rose from Casper's fish and chip shop in Hoyland Common, who happened to mention to another customer that I was writing a book about *Kes*. This was news to me! Although I must admit, Dave's remark certainly sowed a seed in my mind, and it slowly began germination. So, Dave, this is all your fault! As time passed, and I had collected a lot more information and images, a book did indeed become a distinct possibility, and I became more and more focussed on the idea. So, the article became increasingly more expanded, and this is the result. I hope I have succeeded and done the film justice. I truly believe that *Kes* is still worthy of such a book as it is of great cinematic and social history and hopefully will remain so for a long time to come.

An early interest in falconry, again like Billy Casper, catapulted me into a different and amazing world. To this day, I have no idea as to why I became so interested in and took up the art of falconry, unless it was through watching a falconer/taxidermist, John

Bishop Murray, at Wollaton Hall flying a Golden Eagle in the early 1960s, (we will meet John Murray again later in a quite remarkable *Kes* connection) but, yet again, like Billy Casper, it released me from the grind of almost constant boring school-life and gave me a new and revitalised interest like nothing ever had before. As Jarvis Cocker of the band *Pulp*, so eloquently pointed out in an interview with Greg Davies in *Looking for Kes*, Billy had been freed from his jesses and flew ever higher. And so, had I. If my work here does anything at all, I would like it to be the catalyst for reintroducing it back into schools again and to help perpetuate the memory of its author, Barry Hines. That would render my time and research on this project well worthwhile.

[4] The author in 1967 (aged just 19) at his home in Carlton, Nottinghamshire with Eos. [5] Some members of the East Midlands Hawking Club. The author is to the right of the image holding Ajax, his imperial eagle. [6] Jack Lee's female Eurasian kestrel which he flew at Hoyland Common in 1968.

[7] Eos, the author's male Eurasian kestrel, which he flew at Hoyland Common, possibly for *Kes*, in 1968. [8] The Star public house where the author met the producer and cameraman for a filming session (most likely for *Kes*). [9] Front cover of Professor David Forrest's and Sue Vice's book.

Chapter 2

Tankersley Old Hall
& Fish and Chips
(11th August 2021)

After viewing Greg Davies's documentary, *Looking for Kes*, my interest was rejuvenated to say the least and I began to make some preparations for my own visits to the film locations, and I would also base my planned fully illustrated talk on these same known actual film locations, as far as possible. I had decided at the outset, that anything even remotely connected to *Kes* would be grist for the mill and possibly used for this book. This required a great deal of research, and it soon became obvious that to photograph as many of these film locations and other aspects that I would shortly come across, would require far more than a single day in the field. In fact, it took eight wonderful full days and two half days of separate visits to Barnsley, Hoyland Common, Doncaster and Sheffield, spread over the course of almost two years, from August 2021 to May 2023. I made extended notes from Greg's film, plus internet searches of David 'Dai' Bradley's own Kes-BillyCasper.co.uk website, plus the use of the three previously mentioned and highly relevant books. Even so, it took a lot of effort and much driving around to secure the shots that I required to put together the illustrated talk that I hoped would do the story of the film justice.

Many feature films use sets specially constructed for the purpose which are then dismantled and removed after filming is complete, but, as I later discovered, the beauty of *Kes* is that nearly all the film locations were real sites that still exist today, albeit some of them now being barely recognisable from their 1968 appearance. These locations were the tangible reasons that I could perhaps visit, and this aspect really appealed to me and was yet one more of the main reasons that I began my quest. And what is more important, they were all relatively close together and even more of a bonus, were just over an hour's drive from my home in Nottinghamshire. My visits to these locations did not follow the order of the actual film sequences and are repeated here in the order in which they were visited and photographed.

The first part of my plan was to draw up a list of some of the most important locations for my first trip to Hoyland Common, and one of these, for me at least, was the old ruins of Tankersley Old Hall, where Billy Casper takes Kes from an eyrie, or nest, in the crumbling walls. To be perfectly truthful, I was not even sure that the ruins were still present. After all, more than fifty years had lapsed since the film was made and the building was obviously unsafe and in a dilapidated state back then. At least, I knew that the ruins were still there when Greg Davies presented *Looking for Kes*, so I concluded, a visit would be worth the effort. However, I had visit would be worth the effort. However, I had decided at the outset, that if any of the locations no longer existed as shown in the film, I would still photograph whatever was now in their place, simply for the record, and this happened on more than one occasion. Time moves on and waits for nobody, so from the outset, I was prepared for some locations to be virtually unrecognisable due to development or other reasons.

I wrote out a list of three prime film locations, plus other *Kes* related aspects for my first shoot, together with postcodes which I subsequently placed into my satnav. I include them all here for the benefit of fellow *Kes* fans who may wish to follow in my footsteps. The locations are as follows:

1. Tankersley Old Hall, Tankersley. From where Billy obtains Kes (S74 0DX).

2. Bell Ground Wood, Tankersley. The wood which Billy traverses on his way to Tankersley Old Hall to take Kes (S74 0DX).

3. Barry Hines's grave, St. Peter's Church, Tankersley (S74 0DU).

4. Caspers Fish & Chips shop, Princess Street, Hoyland Common (S74 0AA).

5. Barry Hines's house with blue plaque, 78 Hoyland Road, Hoyland Common (S74 0AA).

6. Hoyland Common Working Men's Club, 13 Fitzwilliam Street, Hoyland Common (S74 0NJ).

7. The *Kes* House, 56 Parkside Road, Hoyland Common. The house used as the Casper household in the film (S74 0AH).

There were of course, many other locations that I desperately wanted to photograph, but the above list I knew, would take up most, if not the whole day. So, with my son David, we set off from my home in Nottingham and began the drive up the M1 motorway to Junction 36, where we turned off for the village of Hoyland Common, which is very close to the motorway itself. This reminded me of the same journey that I had made with Jack Lee more than half a century previously to fly our two kestrels for a film producer and cameraman. I had prepared a few rough hand drawn maps to help pinpoint the locations more easily and immediately, these became very useful. My original plan was to drive along Tankersley Lane from Hoyland Common, but Tankersley Lane was blocked off to car traffic due to roadworks. How fortunate that I had previously drawn a map, because by drawing this, I knew beforehand that there was a southern entrance to the track approaching the old hall. We drove down Sheffield Road until we came to a bridge at Lidget, after which we continued for approximately 500 yards until we arrived at a sign for Harley, at which point we turned right onto an unmettled cart-track known as Black Lane and which I knew would take us up to the ruined hall. Unfortunately, we discovered that the road was immediately barred by a locked, yellow painted metal gate together with a notice which stated that it was a private road for residents only. I pulled the car up at the gate and discovered that it was in fact unlocked but decided not to risk going through with the car just in case we might find it locked on the way back and could not get out. At this point I didn't realise that I could have driven all the way up Black Lane and emerge safely at the other end with no risk of being locked in. But without this prior knowledge, I wasn't going to risk it and reversed the car onto the main road and parked up on a triangular patch of grass directly opposite. I collected my camera and we then set off on foot along Black Lane.

It was quite a walk along Black Lane, but it was very pleasant to be out in the countryside in full morning sunshine. The unmade road was flanked by fields and woodlands on both sides, and we had a very enjoyable walk, constantly scanning ahead for signs of the ruined Tankersley Old Hall, because we had no idea as to how far up the track the old hall was situated. We had been walking for quite some time before the ruins came into view for the first time [10]. I remember feeling a real surge of excitement at this point. For more than half a century, I had desired to see this ruined building and now here it was in all its dilapidated glory before my very eyes. Why I had never tried to visit the site years earlier, I have no real idea, except that I must have unconsciously thought that it was a specially built film set which had simply been dismantled after filming ceased, and it was only by viewing *Looking for Kes* with Greg Davies that gave me the knowledge that the old hall was a real, if dilapidated building that actually still existed. I couldn't believe that I was finally viewing this iconic site, the site from where Billy Casper takes his kestrel. I had watched this scene countless times and now I was here too, on site, for real. In the film, this ruin is referred to as Monastery Farm, although it is really known as Tankersley Old Hall. This is a crumbling edifice of a ruin of what once must have been a grand building, and which once belonged to Sir Richard Fanshawe back in the days of the English Civil War.

In the film, as Billy stares at the ruin, a kestrel chooses that moment to fly out and settle on a nearby telephone pole, where it is shortly seen flying in company with another. Billy crosses the dirt-track lane, climbs the low wall and edges towards the crumbling ruin, where he is spotted by the farmer (Eric Bolderson).

"Nah then, what's tha doin?" asks the farmer.

"Now't", says Billy, "Can I 'ave a look at that kestrel's nest?"

The farmer replies, "There's no kestrel's nest here, now clear off."

But Billy answers, "There is, 'ave bin watchin' 'em come and go, feeding young 'uns."

"Aye, they've bin there for years," relents the farmer.

"What would tha do wi it if tha got one?" asks the farmer.

"I'd train it' "says Billy.

"Would tha," says the farmer.

51

"Tha's not many knows about falconry, they're 'ard to train. If they're not kept properly, it's criminal. Besides, the building isn't safe to climb, I won't let my little daughter anywhere near it."

"Does tha know where I can get a book on falconry," asks Billy.

"Tha could try the library in town," replies the farmer.

This scene was very much on my mind as we hurried further along the cart track until we came directly opposite the ruin, which was situated about one hundred yards across a field containing a couple of horses. For me, it was like visiting the Alamo, or Rorke's Drift, or the battlefield of the Little Big Horn, all moments in history which have fascinated me all my life. To say I was ecstatic would be an understatement. I resisted the temptation to do a 'Billy Casper' by climbing over the low wall and was content to use my 400mm Nikon zoom lens to take close-up photographs of the crumbling edifice. Some of the centre sections had fallen since *Kes* was made, but four corner pillars of the building and parts of the walls were still standing, with a few wildflowers growing at their summit. There was a lovely farmhouse next door, and I did think of asking the occupants if we could approach the ruin, but eventually decided against it as I thought that they must get totally fed up with such inane requests from *Kes* fans and I had no desire to add to their possible wrath. I took numerous photographs from various angles, so completing the first location on my list. I couldn't help wondering though, what a shame that in the next few years, the remaining crumbling pillars are likely to come crashing down to earth, leaving just a pile of rubble on the ground. One corner pillar seemed very top heavy; I had particularly noticed this in Greg Davies's documentary *Looking for Kes*. It would be great if it could be reconstructed back to its former condition as it appeared in *Kes*, for it certainly is a great piece of historic cinematic memorabilia. However, due to cost and possibly lack of enthusiasm for the project, this seems unlikely unfortunately.

So, with the first shots in the can, it was time to turn our attention to the second shoot on my list, and for this, we simply had to turn around from Tankersley Old Hall and face Bell Ground Wood which was just opposite and which ran for some distance along Black Lane. In the film, Billy wanders through this very wood and exits by a stile onto the cart-track opposite Tankersley Old Hall [11]. From the stile, he watched the kestrels going in and out of the ruins whilst chewing on a blade of grass and deep in thought, surprised that he had discovered that the small falcons were breeding there. Not long afterwards, he returned to the ruins to take his kestrel, Kes, the namesake of the film. The stile is still there to this day, although it has very recently undergone some much-needed repairs.

Later, in school, Billy suggests to his 'friend', MacDowell (Robert Naylor), to arrange a time to go bird nesting the following morning, as bird nesting was a popular past time back then, now illegal today of course, as indeed it was back in 1968. Another friend, Guthrie (Desmond Guthrie who sadly passed away in 2015) said that he couldn't make it as he was taking his girlfriend out to Sheffield, but at around six in the morning, when Billy calls for him, MacDowell is still asleep in bed, so Billy tosses a few small stones up at the bedroom window to attract his attention, angering MacDowell's Mum (Beryl Carroll) who informs Billy that her son is not coming out as he is still asleep in bed and she tells him to clear off. Having little choice, Billy wanders off alone through the nearby Bell Ground Woods, whacking down weeds with a stick, which he eventually throws into a stagnant pond. He eventually ventures to the far end of the wood and by the stile, gazes across to the old ruin.

Here, I took many images of sections of the wood itself, including part of the track through the wood and some images of the stile itself, which at this, our first visit, was somewhat rickety, so completing stage two of this visit. The wood is a lovely, peaceful place to be, especially on a sunny August day such as this. However, as we only ventured a short distance into the wood through lack of time, I made a mental vow I would return at some future date to walk the full length of the wood, as Billy Casper had done.

The next target was pure guesswork on my part. I knew that Barry Hines had sadly passed away in 2016, but despite numerous attempts to discover the grave location, I could initially find precious little information, either in print, or on the internet. I had seen a photograph of it on the internet, but no location was given. There seemed to be a hint at nearby Oughtibridge, but nothing concrete was forthcoming. By the same token, nothing also seemed to have been added to David Bradley's website, so I drew a blank there too. However, I had read somewhere that Barry had desired to be buried close to his beloved village of Hoyland Common and in the meantime, I had discovered a photograph, again on the internet, which depicted an image of Barry's funeral procession at St. Peter's church Tankersley, which is a mere stones-throw from Hoyland Common [12]. Therefore, I surmised that if Barry's funeral was held at St. Peter's church, it seemed a distinct possibility that his final resting place could also be there. As we were in the vicinity at Tankersley Old Hall, I considered that it was worth a shot, so we made our way on foot further up Black Lane until we met a young couple coming towards us. I asked them if they could confirm that St. Peter's church was ahead of us, and they replied in the affirmative. After another fair walk along this lovely track, and shortly after passing beneath the M1 motorway, the square tower of St. Peter's church presently came into view. As we ventured through the gates and along the church path, I noticed that all the graves were of some vintage, some from the seventeenth century. This did not look too promising, so we ventured further into the church grounds and found that there was a largeish plot of much more recent graves to the rear. This looked more like it. I already knew what the gravestone looked like from the internet image, and from that same image, I also knew that it was beside a stone wall. The latter was plainly obvious, so I headed towards the wall and within seconds, I had found his grave [13]. To say I was elated, in a sad sort of way, would be an understatement, for I never really expected to find it so quickly, if at all, at least not on this first visit. Much to my surprise, the black headstone made no mention of *Kes*, Barry's most famous work. There was however a lovely, engraved image of a Kestrel hovering in flight on the right-hand top corner of the stone [14]. The memorial text read as follows:

> In Loving Memory Of
> BARRY HINES
> 30th June 1939 - 18th March 2016
> AN INSPRIRATIONAL MAN
> BORN AND BRED
> IN HOYLAND COMMON

I took numerous photographs of the grave and also a few of a ceramic kestrel that had been fixed to a tree beside the grave, along with three other ceramics, two of which were blue coloured birds of no particular species, together with nests and eggs [15]. I thought this was a nice touch. I placed two of my copies of *A Kestrel for a Knave* and Richard Hines's *No Way but Gentleness* on the pedestal of Barry's grave and photographed them in this position. This was a red-letter day for me and was as close as I could ever have got to Barry, for unfortunately, I never had the pleasure of meeting him in life. Why is it that we always seem to leave such things too late? However, back then, as indeed now, I had no contact details whatsoever for any members of the cast and crew. Finding Barry's grave was a remarkable and very tangible experience for me and not one that I was likely to forget anytime soon. Some months later, I found more images of Barry's final resting place in the public domain on the internet. Had I found this site earlier, my research would have been so much easier.

Time was now pressing, and we were becoming somewhat hungry, so the obvious next step was to return to Hoyland Common and on to Caspers Fish & Chips shop, which was also high on my list. This I simply couldn't wait for. However, before we could achieve this end, we had to walk all the way back down Black Lane, past Tankersley Old Hall again, where I took a few more photographs, well, one can never have enough images, especially as the sun had moved across the sky somewhat, exposing features in the ruin which had previously been in shadow. Returning to the car, we put in the postcode for the chip shop in the satnav and set off back up Sheffield Road towards Hoyland Common.

Totally unaware of where we were going exactly, I parked the car on Hoyland Road, remarkably, just opposite from the Star public house, where over fifty years previously, Jack Lee and I had taken our kestrels, and which had been the catalyst for this entire project. I took a couple of images of the Star, and it wasn't until I returned home and viewed the images on my laptop that I realised that I had also taken a picture of Tinker Lane where my later research informed me was where both Barry and Richard Hines had previously lived. Facing the lane and standing on Hoyland Road, the Star sits on the left corner of Tinker Lane. So that was a bonus that I hadn't expected. However, at that time,

I had no idea which house, or houses, the brothers had lived in on Tinker Lane, so that was another note for more future research, particularly as I wished to find out more about Barry Hines, especially places where he had lived, primarily because these were tangible.

A short walk along Hoyland Road brought us to Princess Street, although we had spotted the sign for Caspers Fish & Chips long before we reached Princess Street itself [16]. This was a part of Greg Davies's documentary that I hoped to emulate, and I was not to be disappointed. As soon as we entered the shop on Princess Street, I immediately recognised the owner, Dave Rose, and we struck up a warm-hearted friendship [17]. I knew from the documentary that the counter faced the shop doorway instead of to the right, as it appeared in *Kes*, but I have to say it felt surreal to be in the same shop where Billy Casper had spent his brother Jud's hard-earned cash on fish and chips instead of placing the money as bets on the two horses, Crackpot and Tell Him He's Dead, as instructed. Jud had no doubt believed that they would be a wise bet. We both ordered a portion of fish and chips and I can honestly state, David 'Dai' Bradley was right when he said that they "Were bloody good fish and chips."

In *Kes*, we see Billy entering this fish and chips shop on Princess Street and after ordering his chips, Billy asks:

"Got any scraps missus.".

The chip shop owner in the film, Floyd, (Bill Dean 1921-2000) says to his assistant:

"Aye but don't be goin' mad."

Scraps are a delightful Yorkshire term for what we in Nottingham refer to as batter bits, or fish bits, namely the little pieces of batter that fall from deep frying fish. They are very popular, and many people ask for them. Whenever I am in a Yorkshire fish and chips shop, which I have to say is fairly frequently and I hear someone asking for scraps, it always, without fail instantly reminds me of *Kes*, no matter if I have other things on my mind. I have even mentioned this to a few fish shop employees, but most were too young to remember and so, rather unsurprisingly, were unaware of the film; well, it was over half a century ago. They must have thought I was daft in the head! Others though, remembered the film fondly, most saying it was their favourite film ever. I wouldn't argue with that!

Another aspect that I did not expect was that there were several framed photographs from *Kes* which adorned the walls of the chip shop, some of them personally signed by David 'Dai' Bradley. Dave Rose told me that some of these had been a gift from Greg Davies's film crew as a thank you for the time spent filming there. It was such a lovely gesture and added to the aura of the film in the shop. Additionally, there was also a stuffed Little Owl in a glass case in the shop window. I mused, what a shame it wasn't the dead kestrel that had been used in the final film sequences. Wouldn't that have been something? (I was to discover much more about the dead kestrel later.) I remember David Bradley saying that as well as the counter change, the windows had been rendered smaller, the faint outlines of the previous windows were still visible in the exterior pebble dashing, the latter of which had also apparently been added since 1968. I took many photographs of both the interior and exterior of the shop and Dave gladly consented to having his photograph taken with me both inside and outside [18]. The exterior of the shop previously had a lighted display box which informed passers-by that the shop was called The Harbour, and this latter signage was still present when Greg Davies presented his documentary. This had since recently been changed to commemorate the film and now depicted a photograph of Barry Hines and several small images of David Bradley, one showing the famous 'V' sign [19]. The lettering on the sign reads:

CASPERS FISH & CHIPS
The Fish & Chip Shop from the Barry Hines Film Kes
Starring David Bradley as Billy Casper
Tel: 07432 142 798

This shop was one of only two memorials that were known to me concerning *Kes* that were currently visible in Hoyland Common today (although a third one is now planned) and it is a sad reflection that the local council have not capitalised on this phenomenal book and film.

The film was eventually judged the 7th best British film of all time. For the record, here are those ten best British films of all time, voted for by The British Film Institute:

1. *The Third Man* (1949)
2. *Brief Encounter* (1945)
3. *Lawrence of Arabia* (1962)
4. *The 39 Steps* (1935)
5. *Great Expectations* (1946)
6. *Kind Hearts & Coronets* (1949)
7. *Kes* (1969)
8. *Don't Look Now* (1973)
9. *The Red Shoes* (1948)
10. *Trainspotting* (1996)

Had it been left to me, *Kes* would have been at number one on this list and for a great many others too I suspect. It certainly put Barnsley and Hoyland Common on the map, so why have the respective councils largely ignored it? In 1971, *Kes* was awarded two BAFTA awards (British Academy of Film and Television Arts). The first one was awarded for Best Supporting Actor (Colin Welland) and the second for Most Promising Newcomer to Leading Film Roles (David 'Dai' Bradley). So much for the naysayers and critics who predicted the film would flop.

The next stage of our excursion was to find and photograph Barry Hines's house which I knew had recently received a blue plaque in his honour. Although this house did not feature in *Kes*, it was one of many related aspects for the whole *Kes* story that I eventually discovered and photographed. Dave Rose was most helpful in guiding us to this, and three other sites on my list. For Barry Hines's former house, we literally had to retrace our steps up Princess Street, back on to Hoyland Road and the house was plainly visible a hundred yards or so along Hoyland Road on the left [20]. The house is number 78 Hoyland Road and the bright blue plaque reads [21]:

> THE YORKSHIRE SOCIETY
> BARRY HINES
> 1939 - 2016
> Author of 'A Kestrel for a Knave'
> and other novels which gave a
> voice to working-class
> people, lived here.
> 1970-1976.

1970 was of course two years after Barry published *A Kestrel for Knave*, but that didn't matter, it was again, still something tangible and, of course, was duly photographed. 1970 was however, the year that *Kes* was officially released, and Barry Hines was living here at this address at that time. The house was an end terrace built in lovely buff coloured stone and I am grateful to The Yorkshire Society and members of the Kes Group for providing this accolade to a great author.

The next location was Fitzwilliam Street, which necessitated a walk back down Princess Street, past Caspers Fish & Chips for a hundred yards or so until we came to Fitzwilliam Street on our right [22]. This was a favourite haunt of Barry Hines, who regularly visited the Hoyland Common Working Men's Club which was situated on the left-hand side near the bottom of the long, slightly sloping street, at No. 13 [23 & 24]. Here, Barry often sat of an evening listening to the tales of the locals and as aforementioned, apparently many of these characters and their stories ended up in his novels. I photographed the exterior of the premises and hoped to venture inside, but unfortunately it was closed at the time, so I decided that another visit would have to wait for some future date. However, it wasn't overly important because it didn't feature in *Kes*, although it did feature in Greg Davies's *Looking for Kes*, and it was a frequent haunt of Barry Hines, so these aspects gave it a *Kes* connection for me. I also required some images of Fitzwilliam Street itself, for in the film, we see Billy Casper walking up this street, which still looks virtually the same today, except for the fact that there are a great many more parked cars here than there was in 1968. In fact, as I was to discover, Fitzwilliam Street is probably the only *Kes* film location that has scarcely changed at all since 1968. The same terraced houses that line the street on both sides are still there. Billy had obtained his meat for Kes from the mobile butcher's van which the film crew parked here for the scene. Whilst wandering about eating his fish and chips, Billy ventures along Fitzwilliam Street, and not far from the chip shop itself, he approaches the butcher's van. He offers the owner (Leslie Stringer) some of his chips as he parcels up some meat for Billy.

"Still got that bird then," asks the butcher.

"Yup," replies Billy.

"Well, you can have these pieces of meat for nothing, they're only scraps."

Billy is amazed: "For now't, thanks."

The final shoot of the day concerned the location of Billy Casper's house. This house, 56 Parkside Road, was situated not far from Fitzwilliam Street and was used by the film crew as the Casper household where Billy, Jud (Freddie Fletcher) and his mother (Lynne Perrie) lived [25]. According to David Bradley's website, the property was owned by Connie and Duggie Howarth and in return for the film crew's use, the entire house was refurbished, which was a wonderful gesture. We soon found the property but did not disturb the occupants and took three or four shots with my telephoto lens. For some now forgotten reason, I resisted the temptation to venture around to the rear of the property where a mews had been constructed by the film crew carpenters to house Kes, and where also the catering van was positioned for the use of cast and crew. This oversight was corrected on a later visit.

We get an early impression of Billy's older brother, Jud, as soon as the film begins. They are both sharing a small bed in a darkened room when the clock alarm bell rings. Billy tries to wake up Jud as he must get up to work at the colliery. Billy shouts out:

"Jud, wake up, tha'll be late for work."

But at first Jud refuses to budge and clouts Billy.

"Gi' over, I'm tellin me Mam on thee," moans Billy.

"Shut it then," yells Jud.

Jud eventually rises but cruelly makes Billy get up and turn off the light after leaving the room. Billy gets up shortly afterwards because he must do a paper round before going off to school. Unfortunately for Billy, because Jud was late getting up, he takes Billy's bike, leaving Billy to complete his paper round on foot.

"Bloody 'ell fire, he's nicked me bleedin' bike," yells Billy.

The newsagent, Mr. Porter, (Harry Markham 1906-1981) has a go at Billy for being late but when Billy tells him that Jud has nicked his bike, he has little sympathy and wonders how he will complete his paper round in time to get back to school. Billy tells the newsagent he knows some short-cuts.

It had been a highly successful day with all the required images safely in the camera. The next job was to organise a second journey once I had selected more locations to place on film, before driving back through Hoyland Common and onto the M1 for the journey back to Nottingham.

[10] Tankersley Old Hall. [11] The stile at the edge of Bell Ground Wood that Billy Casper crosses on his way to take Kes from Tankersley Old Hall. [12] St. Peter's church. [13] Barry Hines's grave at St. Peter's church. [14] The hovering kestrel engraved on Barry Hines's gravestone. [15] Ceramic kestrel beside the grave. [16] Caspers Fish & Chips shop signage on the corner of Princess Street and Hoyland Road. [17] Dave Rose (left) and the author (right) inside Caspers Fish & Chips shop. [18] Entrance to Caspers Fish & Chips shop. [19] Main signage for Caspers Fish & Chips shop as seen on Princess Street. [20] The former home of Barry Hines at No. 78 Hoyland Road. [21] The blue plaque at No.78 Hoyland Road. [22] Fitzwilliam Street, Hoyland Common. Billy Casper is seen walking up this street in *Kes*. It is also the location of the mobile butcher's van from where Billy obtains his meat for Kes. [23] Hoyland Common Working Men's Club at No. 13 Fitzwilliam Street. Barry Hines often visited the club and acquired stories here for his novels. The club also featured in the Greg Davies's documentary *Looking for Kes*. [24] Another view of Hoyland Common Working Men's Club. [25] No. 56 Parkside Road. This was the location of the Casper household in *Kes*.

Chapter 3

The Caning & That Football Match
(3rd February 2022)

Once I had sorted through the images of the first *Kes* shoot, I realised that I would need to return to some of the locations that we had already covered because I required some different angles of the same subject. I also added some new locations that I had researched, and so my second shoot list reads as follows:

1. Fitzwilliam Street, Hoyland Common. I realised that I had taken shots looking down the street, but not upwards, as shown in the film (S74 0NJ).

2. Caspers Fish & Chips shop. I needed more exterior shots (S74 0AA).

3. The Betting Shop, 252a Pontefract Road in nearby Lundwood. Barnsley, (now called Todays Express) where Billy fails to place Jud's bets (S71 5PN).

4. Lewis Road, where Billy meets the milkman, Duggie Brown (S71 5HY).

5. St. Helen's School, 41 St. Helens Way, Monk Bretton, Barnsley. The school that I originally believed to be Billy's and David Bradley's school, but this, as I later discovered was not the case (S71 2PS).

6. The Cudworth Hotel/The Dard's, Cudworth. Site of Jud's and Mrs. Casper's night out (S72 8SU).

7. Skier's Spring Colliery, Broadcarr Road, Hoyland. Site of Jud's workplace at the coal mine (S74 9BU).

8. Grange View, Blacker Hill, near Hoyland Common on the A6195. Site of the old coking plant where Billy reads the *Dandy* comic (S74 0RB).

Again, my son David accompanied me as we set off on a cold, but gloriously sunny day, turning off at Junction 36 of the M1 motorway. We began the day by searching for Grange View on Blacker Hill, and to achieve this end we took the A6195 out of Hoyland Common for about a mile or so and soon came into view of Blacker Hill **[26]**. This is the site where Billy Casper reads his *Dandy* comic during his newspaper round. In the film, Billy sits before a huge, industrial, clanking, and smoke billowing coking plant, reading from a comic strip concerning Desperate Dan, a character that I well remember from my own school days. I knew that the site had changed dramatically, as it was shown as such in Greg Davies's documentary *Looking for Kes*. Both he and David 'Dai' Bradley were filmed sitting on a roadside barrier filmed sitting on a roadside barrier with the former site in the background. The area was now rural and consisted of green fields, all traces of heavy industry having long since been eradicated. A great improvement. We soon found the site and pulled up in a layby which was quite close to where Greg and David were filmed. However, since then, saplings had grown up behind the road barriers somewhat obscuring the view, so to obtain clearer photographs, I had to drive a short distance further along the road, take a left turn and park up on a grass verge. This viewpoint was virtually the same and very picturesque, several photographs were taken from this location. Without prior knowledge nobody would ever have been aware that a huge coking plant had existed here previously, the site has changed enormously and is very pleasant and rural today. At least, we were not bothered by the heavy and constant stream of traffic that rushed by on the main road as Greg and David had been.

After leaving this lovely scene, we followed the road for a short distance until we passed a churchyard on our right and I wondered if this was the same churchyard mentioned in David 'Dai' Bradley's website, where Mr. Farthing (Colin Welland) disturbs Billy flying Kes. Although I had not yet properly researched this site, I hoped for the best and performed a rather rapid about turn and drove through the churchyard entrance, parking up by the church itself. According to a brief resume I had made of the website, we had to walk through the cemetery and at the end of the path we would find the field. I was not sure if this was the exact location, for there was a railway line beyond the fence at the conclusion of the cemetery, which did not seem right, but there was a field to the right of the cemetery, and I wondered if this was the place. I had my doubts, but I took a few images simply because we were there, and I could always delete them afterwards if this was the wrong site. I discovered on arrival home that this indeed was not the original site. The real one would now have to be properly researched and added to my list for a return visit.

We then took the A628 and drove on to nearby Lundwood, where several scenes from *Kes* were filmed. Not far along the road from the betting shop was Lewis Road. This was the location for the milkman, Duggie Brown (Lynne Perrie's brother in real life) who was sat in his milk float near the bottom of this short road [27]. This is where Billy tells Duggie, "Tha can go faster on a kid's scooter than that old ransack" (of a milk float).

Billy steals a bottle of orange juice and a carton of eggs from the milk float and has the cheek and audacity to replace the empty juice bottle back in a crate as Duggie drives off. This road has changed little since 1968 and I took several photographs here [28].

Sadly, Duggie Brown passed away in August 2022, he was a successful and much-loved comedian.

I understand this was also the village where the late Brian Glover once lived for a time. Brian was an actor, a teacher, and a wrestler and was someone who I would have loved to have met. I am not normally someone who admires so-called celebrities, and never put them on pedestals, but Brian seemed so down to earth and natural, with no airs and graces. Brian also did voice-overs for television commercials, for example: "Tetley make tea bags, make tea" and for Allinson's bread: "Bread wi' nowt teken out," all in his wonderful broad Yorkshire dialect which I love. He also, amongst other programmes, appeared in *Porridge* and *Last of the Summer Wine*, although *Kes* was his first credited film role, and he played the amazing part of the bullying PE teacher, Mr. Sugden, and what a great part he played too. The football scenes in *Kes* were, for me at least, the best football match scenes ever filmed in British cinematic history.

However, to return to my quest, the next port of call was the betting shop on Pontefract Road in Lundwood, where Billy failed to place Jud's bets on two horses. The betting shop was easily found, after passing a row of shops on the left-hand side of the main road [29]. The bright scarlet colouration of the fascia boards particularly made the shop stand out from the other buildings in the road. I photographed the exterior from two different angles, but we didn't venture inside. It is no longer a betting shop and is now known as Today's Express, but at least it is still there today. Despite the shop's more modern look, it is easily recognisable as the betting shop in *Kes*.

In the film, returning from school, Billy enters the mews to prepare food for Kes. Here he finds a note from Jud, together with some money to place a bet on two horses, Crackpot and Tell Him He's Dead. This annoys Billy, but he knows he must do it because he does not want to anger Jud, who is not known for his good humour, so he sets off for the betting shop. He enters the shop and approaches the counter, where a young lady, (this was Julie Goodyear, Bet Lynch of *Coronation Street* fame, although I doubt anyone would recognise her because she was shown basically in silhouette) asks Billy if she can help him. He declines the offer and instead, he approaches a man (Ted Carroll, who sadly died in 1998) studying racing form from a newspaper. Billy presumed that this was the man to ask about Jud's chances with the two horses, so he asks him for advice. The man studies the two horses in his paper, but then tells Billy that he doesn't much rate their chances, "Bin lookin at these two meself, one is okay and will do well if it wins, t'other one no chance, but can't see it meself," he exclaims.

"Great," says Billy and sets off at once to spend some of Jud's hard-earned cash. Billy obviously thinks that if the horses don't win, Jud will be none the wiser and would have lost the money anyway. It never enters Billy's head for a moment that they might just win and then suffer the revenge that Jud will take if they do. Later in the day, Billy wanders on, back in Lundwood again, where he passes the betting shop, where the owner is just locking up the premises.

"Ave ya seen our Jud?" Billy asks the owner.

"I see *you* haven't, you're still in one piece," came the reply.

"Why, did they win?" asks Billy.

"Did they win! did they win! he'd have won a tenner at least, he nearly smashed up the shop 'till we managed to convince him you didn't place any bets."

"Bloody 'ell fire," mutters Billy, and heads off back to school, where he cannot concentrate on his maths lesson. He is now terrified of what Jud will do to him. Looking out of the classroom window, Billy suddenly spies an angry looking Jud striding rapidly across the school grounds, searching for Billy. The colour fades from Billy's already pale face and he shrinks behind his desk. The maths teacher (Geoffrey Banks – who died 2008) asks Billy if he is unwell and would he like to go out and get a drink of water.

"No thanks sir, I'm alreet," answers Billy shakily.

Jud next appears outside the classroom door window, shaking his fist at Billy. The maths teacher notices Jud and asks Billy:

"Isn't that your illustrious brother out there? I didn't think he was the type to pay his old school a visit."

Billy is visibly shaken and crouches further beneath his desk, just as the school bell sounds. Billy waits until the class is empty and crawls out from his hiding place behind the desk and darts outside, avoiding Jud who is quizzing some kids in the corridor.

"I'll kill the little bastard when I get my 'ands on him."

Billy seeks a new hiding place and eventually disappears inside the toilet block. But Billy soon realises the toilets are too obvious a place in which to hide and so he darts outside and settles down in the dark, dank recesses of the school boiler room. Jud meanwhile continues his search. Thinking Billy might be hiding in the boy's toilets, Jud ventures inside, kicking open each toilet door in turn, hoping to discover Billy, but all he finds is one of Billy's classmates sat on the loo. This was Peter Clegg, otherwise known as Cleggie, although he is not seen on camera.

"Ave you seen our Billy," asks Jud.

"Aye, he's on 'ere wi me," comes the sarcastic reply.

Jud grabs the lad and threatens him with violence. Of course, Billy knows that he cannot stay hidden forever and must face Jud sooner or later, so he eventually emerges from the boiler house. Leaving his hiding place, Billy gingerly enters the school corridor where he is immediately spotted by Mr. Gryce, who shouts at him:

"Where have you been Casper, I've had staff and prefects looking all over for you."

"Nowhere Sir," whimpers Billy.

"Nowhere! are you the invisible man, where are you supposed to be?"

"Ave to see the youth employment officer sir."

"Well get along then, and heaven help your future employer," growls Mr. Gryce.

Billy rushes off to his meeting with the youth employment officer (Bernard Atha – 1928-2022), for which he is late. When he is called from the waiting room, Billy walks straight into the interview room and is immediately told to get out and knock first. Billy does as he is bid, and because he is late, the employment officer initially thinks he is a pupil called Walker, until Billy corrects him. Billy is like a cat on hot bricks and cannot seem to settle, and with good reason, for he is still worrying about Jud. He shows no interest in the proceedings and simply wants to be away. The youth employment officer attempts to discover Billy's interests or hobbies and asks what Billy would like to do for a job, as he needs to be thinking about it as he will be leaving school soon. Billy doesn't know what he wants to do, as he doesn't even like school, but as he says, "At least at work, I will be be gettin' paid for not likin' it."

Asking if he would like an office job, Billy says: "I'll be alreet in an office, 'ave a job to read and write."

Trying another tactic, he asks Billy about mining, at which Billy almost throws a complete tantrum: "Am not goin' darn pit, I wouldn't be seen dead darn pit."

Billy gets up to leave, but the officer calls him back to give him some papers to study, then allows him to go. Billy of course, still has Jud weighing heavily on his mind. Besides, he also has Kes to feed and fly, so he reluctantly makes his way home.

Next on the list was the school where Billy Casper attended, as also did David 'Dai' Bradley in real life. The school that was used in Greg Davies's documentary, The Carlton Academy, was not the same school that was used in *Kes*, for this school was rebuilt on a new site nearby. The original school used in the film, I originally thought, was at Monk Bretton, but I was unaware at this time that the real school was at nearby Athersley South. I had decided at the outset that I wanted the exact original location, or as near as I could get to it at least, even if the school had been demolished, which was apparently the case. The Edward Sheerien School had been built on the same site apparently, but this was also demolished in 2011. Imagine my surprise then when I discovered that at least the St. Helen's Primary School was still there and, what I took to be the same site too at Monk Bretton, and from comparison with a still monochrome photograph taken in 1968 whilst *Kes* was being filmed, the school design was comparable to this still existing primary school. This school was built on very similar lines to the one used in *Kes* and therefore I planned to use the image in this book purely as a comparison to demonstrate what the original school looked like. As with most schools these days, the gates were locked, a sign of the times sadly, but nevertheless, I managed to poke my lens through the railings and took a couple of shots of the building **[30]**. This really made my day, for I was not expecting this at all. Today this school is surrounded by a housing estate. I know, because I had to walk all the way round the estate before I could obtain a worthwhile image of most of the school.

The real St. Helen's Secondary Modern school in nearby South Athersley had played a large part in *Kes*, where many sequences were filmed, and which is why I particularly desired to photograph the location, unfortunately for me, Monk Bretton was the wrong location, so at some stage, this would need to be corrected. One of the sequences in *Kes* concerned Casper's fight in the playground. In school, Billy suffers from concentration, he finds school boring, and this is unsurprising, for the system fails him and besides, he now has his newly acquired kestrel to occupy his waking hours and thoughts. He also has trouble with his bullying classmate MacDowell (Robert Naylor) who, since Billy obtained Kes and now having a far greater interest in something other than thieving, has subsequently left MacDowell's gang. MacDowell takes umbrage at this and insults Billy and pushes him around in the playground, at the same time deriding his mother and brother. Despite MacDowell having his bullying mates around him, Billy retaliates and throws lumps of coke at him scavenged from a large heap near the boiler house. This enrages MacDowell which then develops into a full-scale confrontation and soon, both are battling it out and punching each other on top of the heap of coke, scattering it all over the place. Billy gives as good as he gets and soon both are filthy from rolling about, fighting on the heap of coke, scattering ever more lumps of the stuff all over the playground. As usual, with most school fights, the melee soon attracts the attention of all the other pupils, who charge towards the pair shouting encouragement to both contestants. The resulting noise ensures that the scrap doesn't last long before the kindly Mr. Farthing (Colin Welland – 1934-2015) hears the commotion and intervenes, separating the pair, at the same time, clearing off all the other kids to the four corners of the school. Once Mr. Farthing learns the reasons for the fight, he has a go at MacDowell and shows him what it is like to be bullied and pokes him in the chest. MacDowell backs off and obviously doesn't like this and threatens to bring his dad up to school, to which Mr. Farthing responds:

"Oh yes, and I'll bring my dad too and my dad's heavyweight champion of the world, my dad is, so what will your dad do then, eh? This is what it is like to be bullied. Don't like it do you?"

Smelling tobacco on MacDowell's breath he accuses him of smoking as well as bullying, which MacDowell strongly denies. Nevertheless, he tells MacDowell, "See me after school and clear up this mess."

Mr. Farthing then turns to Billy and asks him about things at home and why he is always in trouble.

"Don't know sir, they always seem to pick one me. Whenever there's any trouble on t'estate, police always come round to our house. Anyway, I 'ent bin in trouble, not since last time. And teacher's sir, they're not bothered about us, and we're not bothered about them."

Billy becomes visibly upset and Mr. Farthing tells him to calm down. This is the point in the film which reminded me of many of my own teachers and how they weren't bothered whether we succeeded or failed. I endured a very similar fight with a bully at my secondary school, but I didn't have the luxury of a kindly Mr. Farthing. Instead, I was grabbed by the teacher by the scruff of the neck and frogmarched off to a classroom to receive three strokes of the cane across the palms of both hands. I later told my grandson Joshua about this episode, and he couldn't believe that teachers were allowed to cane us back then. Some teachers took a personal liking for using the cane and used it at every opportunity.

As aforementioned, before acquiring Kes, Billy used to hang round with MacDowell's gang, often getting into trouble with the police for breaking and entering, shoplifting and other petty crimes. Since Kes came into his life, Billy had found a new partnership to focus on and so left the gang to concentrate on taking Kes out into the countryside to fly her. This was much more to Billy's liking, but MacDowell and his cronies didn't see it this way at all and tended to pick on Billy at almost every opportunity, but this latter fight in the playground episode piqued Mr. Farthing's interest in Billy.

Back in class, the subject arises when Mr. Farthing asks the pupils to tell him about individual facts that have happened to them that are true. Mr. Farthing is one of those rare teachers who realised that we all have potential, if given the chance and opportunity to exercise it and this lesson was a good case in point. Two or three of the class gave examples, one being of by one of the girls (Julie Shakespeare) who tells the class that they were at a party, making a lot of noise and when one of the neighbours complained and threatened to fetch the police; they cheekily told the neighbour to do so, and so the neighbour did! This raised a few laughs from the rest of the class. Mr. Farthing then turns to Billy.

"Now then Casper, can you give us an example of a fact that has happened to you?"

"No sir," says Billy.

But Mr. Farthing doesn't want to let this go.

"Surely, there must be something?"

Billy, somewhat crestfallen, stares blankly at his desk and says nothing.

"Well, nobody is leaving until you come up with something," Mr. Farthing bluntly states. Eventually, Tibbutt (David Glover), one of his classmates, not wishing to remain in class any longer than necessary, pipes up:

"Tell him about tha 'awk" says Tibbut.

Another classmate, George Speed, butts in.

"He's mad o'er it sir, he doesn't bother with anyone else, just his awk."

"Aw, shut thee face, it's better than thee anyroad" yells Billy.

This intrigues Mr. Farthing, who not only states that if anyone else makes a sound that it will also be the last thing they ever do, but he also asks Billy to stand up and give a talk about his hawk. Billy looks embarrassed and again stares blankly at his desktop. Mr. Farthing beckons Billy to the front of the class and asks him again to tell everyone about his bird. Initially, Billy is nervous, but soon gets into his stride and when he mentions jesses, swivel and leash, Mr. Farthing asks him to write these details on the blackboard, as Mr. Farthing has never heard of them. Billy then becomes more confident and talks at some length about how he trained Kes and then exclaimed:

"It were great, she flew to me like a rocket and swooped up into t'air and grabbed meat on t' lure, and that's it then sir, she were trained and there was nowt else I could do."

This also illustrates the point that now Billy has trained Kes, there is indeed nothing further to be done with her, other than continuing flying her to the lure for pure enjoyment and exercise, since kestrels are of little use for the pursuit of natural game, as is the norm with other hawk species trained for falconry purposes. Even so, Mr. Farthing and the whole class were enthralled. This was Billy's moment to shine, and he made the most of it. Mr. Farthing asks Billy if he could come and watch him fly Kes sometime; Billy merely nods. At lunchtime, Billy goes home to take Kes out into the fields to fly her. Several different fields were used in the making of this film, but this one is across the road from St. Peter's church in Hoyland Common. It is now a sports field but differs little from the days when *Kes* was filmed there all those years ago. Kes is stooping well to the lure when Mr. Farthing turns up unexpectedly.

"Bloody 'ell fire," mutters Billy.

"You'll 'ave to stand over there sir and keep quiet," he shouts to Mr. Farthing.

"I won't say a word," he replies, and marvels at the aerial manoeuvres of this lovely little falcon, backed by the haunting music of composer, John Cameron. Once Kes takes the lure and the flying session is over, Billy wanders over to Mr. Farthing to give him a closer look at Kes.

"The most exciting thing I've ever seen in my life," states Mr. Farthing.

Mr. Farthing then returns with Billy to Billy's home to see where he keeps the bird. Soon, both Billy and Mr. Farthing are sitting in the mews, watching Kes and speaking in hushed tones, sitting in a pocket of silence, as Barry Hines so beautifully described it, almost as though it was a privilege to just be allowed to be there and study the bird. Mr. Farthing asks Billy what his mates think about Kes.

"I'm not bothered about them, they talk daft, they say, look, there's Billy Casper wi' his pet 'awk. I could shout at 'em sir; it's not a pet, hawks are not pets, they're manned. Or when folks stop me an' say, is it tame? Is it 'eck tame, it's trained, that's all. It's fierce an' its wild, an' it's not bothered about anybody, not even about me reet. And that's why it's great."

Mr. Farthing replies, "You are probably right Billy; you are probably right."

70

Still concerning the school, we soon become aware of a typical secondary school interlude that was commonplace during my years at school. Namely, receiving the cane as a punishment for misdemeanours. The next day, after his early morning paper round, Billy attends the morning assembly at school. Billy is tired after getting up so early, is bored with the goings-on in assembly and soon his mind wanders, and he has flashbacks from previously when he was out in the fields flying Kes. He becomes totally engrossed in his thoughts and doesn't realise that all the other pupils have now sat back down on the assembly floor, he is still seeing Kes in his mind's eye, flying over the fields, but this leaves him standing visibly alone. This point is not lost on the school's headmaster Mr. Gryce, (played by Bob Bowes – 1922-1979) who is of the old school type and is a strict disciplinarian. He screams at Billy and orders him to his office. All the kids suddenly have a coughing fit which sends Mr. Gryce into a fit of apoplexy. He orders them all to stop this infernal racket and to do their coughing before coming to assembly. The room falls silent, then somebody else coughs. This was too much for Mr. Gryce, who orders the person responsible to own up. Of course, nobody dares to own up. He orders a teacher, Mr. Hesketh, (who died in December 2012) (he was also David 'Dai' Bradley's form teacher in real life) to find the boy responsible and picks on MacDowell. Mr. Gryce shouts out:

"MacDowell, it was you, I might have known, get to my office and God help you boy."

MacDowell tries to proclaim his innocence, but it is futile, and Mr. Hesketh (his real name too, although in the book he is known as Mr. Crossley, he was allowed to use his real name due to Equity reasons) drags MacDowell out into the isle at the side of the assembly room and sends him off to Mr. Gryce's office. The assembly then continues, while a small group of miscreants, including some members of the smoker's union, assemble to await Mr. Gryce's pleasure outside the office. While they stand chatting, a little boy from the 1st year joins them to bring a message from a teacher for Mr. Gryce. MacDowell and his cronies, including Billy, grab the poor little mite and threaten him with violence if he refuses to store their stash of cigarettes in his pockets. Realising he has no choice, the angelic little lad (Martin Harley – born in 1956) does as he is requested but says.

"You'll have to give me something."

One of the bully's then chimes in, "Th'all get some fist if tha don't."

Then they all duly await their respective punishments.

The character of Mr. Gryce, was based on a real-life headmaster named Mr. Hopkins, who was headmaster at nearby Longcar Central School, where Barry Hines and Brian Glover [31] also taught for a time. He was known to be a particularly fierce headmaster and both students and staff alike apparently feared him. Bob Bowes was actually a headmaster in real life, but not at St. Helen's, which is no doubt why he played the character so well. I understand *Kes* was Bob Bowes's only acting role. My own headmaster was very similar and was someone who wouldn't think twice about using the cane on us, so I could sympathise with the kids awaiting their punishment. I have stood outside my headmaster's office more than once, fully expecting a dose of the cane, and usually got it. Mr. Gryce (the kids referred to him as Gryce pudding) begins by reading them the riot act.

"You never listen! Yours is the generation that never listens. Every time it's the same old faces. I taught some of your fathers and I thought, with this fine school and its modern facilities, this behaviour would cease, but no, time and time again, I must use the cane!"

He smells smoke on MacDowell's breath.

"You've been smoking," screams Mr. Gryce.

"No, I haven't," pleads MacDowell.

"Yes, you have, I'll bet you are already looking forward to smoking behind the toilets at breaktime! Turn out your pockets! All of you, come on, turn out your pockets."

The little boy interjects, "Please sir, I've come to bring a message."

He is cut short by Mr. Gryce. This was Ken Loach at his best who had instructed Bob Bowes to ignore the lad if he protests.

"Come on boy, turn out your pockets!"

The little boy is getting worried.

"But please sir, you don't understand."

Mr. Gryce is now getting really annoyed with him.

"Do as you are told boy, turn out your pockets."

The little lad reluctantly turns out his pockets and Mr. Gryce is flabbergasted when he sees all the cigarettes and matches that he places on the table.

"Ah, a regular little smoking factory," Mr. Gryce exclaims.

"Come on, the rest of you, turn out your pockets!"

When he discovers that none of the other lads have any cigarettes, he exclaims loudly, "I don't believe it; I just don't believe it!"

As he turns his back on the pupils and stares out of the window, muttering oaths, the kids begin to laugh, but not for long. Mr. Gryce turns and the boy's line up to receive their caning, which many viewers of the film may not realise, was for real. The boys were really caned and received the equivalent of fifty pence per stroke, although other accounts place the fee at one pound per stroke, but, as I have not yet met any of the cast or crew to verify one or the other, the latter is anyone's guess. At least, they got paid for their pain, which I never did! Apparently, after the first strokes of the cane, the pupils were allowed to don gloves and their gloved hands were placed just out of camera shot. As for the little lad, Martin Harley's tears were for real, and he apparently never forgave the crew. He felt really let down, poor boy. But director Ken Loach wanted realism from his actors, most of whom were ordinary local people who had never acted before except perhaps on the school stage. Therefore, this is precisely why Ken had previously instructed the headmaster to ignore Martin Harley's remonstrances and to interrupt him each time he tried to protest. This was the way Ken Loach worked and was how he obtained his realism from his actors, and it wasn't the only time that he employed such tactics during the making of *Kes*, as we shall see.

The next school sequence, for me personally, was one of the highlights of *Kes*. Which is rather strange, for I am no football fan. This football match, in my limited opinion, was the best football match ever screened in British cinematic history, and I am not alone here. I have never had any love for football, and even less for cricket, but I can watch this scene repeatedly because it is again, so comical and so true to my own life at school on the sports field. Billy's class are getting into their PE kit ready for the game, but Billy is still fully clothed when the games master Mr. Sugden (Brian Glover) spots him and asks Billy why he has not changed into football gear. Billy states that his mum says that he must be excused PE.

"Where's tha note then Casper."

"Aven't got one sir."

This does not impress Mr. Sugden, who brusquely states that a pupil, wishing to be excused PE must, *at the time of the lesson,* provide a note signed by either a parent or guardian to excuse that pupil. Billy obviously had no such note and consequently, had no choice other than begin to get himself ready for PE. Mr. Sugden lends Billy a pair of his own shorts that are several sizes too large. They extended below his knees and covered his entire chest, just like the one's I had at school. Mr. Sugden tells Billy to roll them down, which he does and keeps them up with his own snake belt. Snake belts used to be very popular back in the day, I had a couple myself. They were elasticated and fastened with a metal clasp in the 'S' shape of a curled snake.

Most secondary school children back then came from relatively poor, working-class backgrounds. Although there was a welfare state at that time in Britain, the country was still reeling from the post-war era, with money being a scarce commodity, so how we all managed financially I never found out. What we didn't have, we didn't miss, I guess. I didn't realise this at the time because everyone we knew around us was in the same boat, we were all relatively poor, financially at least, just like Billy Casper and his family, so items such as my football boots for example, were hand-me-downs from an uncle who had long since left school. They were as hard as granite, with nails from the studs poking through the soles into my feet and were at least three sizes too large for me. I tried hammering the nails flat on a cobbler's last that my father owned, (which I still possess to this day), but I could still feel the bumps as I ran about the goal mouth in them. My shorts too were no better. I could have got two other kids inside them with me and still have had room to spare, not that my uncle was obese, he wasn't, he was just a lot taller than me. They reached from well below my knees almost up to my chin. I had to fold them over and keep them up with the elasticated snake belt, exactly like Billy Casper did in *Kes*. Because of my interest in natural history and lack of interest in the game, I would often wander off from the goalmouth (I was usually placed in goal) after some insect or bird that had caught my attention and then, because of my wandering and absence from the pitch, let in a goal, which never went down too well with either staff or pupils. *Kes* brought all these memories flooding back home to me in real terms because they were so amazingly like my own school life on the football pitch. As stated earlier, for me, *Kes* was not just a film, it was real. *Kes* had this electrifying, close to home effect on me, and partially explained why my teachers behaved the way they did.

Then it was out onto the football field, where the teams were being assembled. Brian was in his element here as Mr. Sugden, for he played team captain, commentator, referee, and other roles in football which are alien to me, but which were obviously associated with the game. And he wouldn't take no for an answer, from anyone. He picked most of the best players for his team, much to the wrath of the boys in the other team. Mr. Sugden took off his red tracksuit to reveal the gleaming scarlet colours of his Manchester United strip. The other team decided to become Tottenham Hotspur. A couple of the lads were questioning Mr. Sugden when he blurted:

"Are you trying to tell me how to play football lad?"

Another lad asked Mr. Sugden if he was going to play Denis Law this week and he replied, "No," showing his white number nine on his shirt.

"Don't you know your numbers lad, I'm Bobby Charlton today, besides, Denis Law's in t' wash."

Just like me, Billy was the last of the line-up to be picked, standing alone where previously there was a long line of boys. He eventually found himself on Mr. Sugden's team.

"Come on lad, I've *got* to have you!"

Again, to Billy's dismay, Mr. Sugden places Billy in goal which doesn't go down well with Billy at all and soon he begins playing about by climbing up onto the goal crossbar and begins swinging like an ape from it. Mr. Sugden spies him and says, "Casper! what's tha doin?"

"Nowt sir, and for my next trick."

"Trick, I'll give you trick lad," shouts Mr. Sugden.

Unfortunately for Billy, he fails to save a shot from Tottenham Hotspur, rendering the score so far: Tottenham Hotspur 1, Manchester United 0. Mr. Sugden is furious with Billy, as he thinks Billy let the goal in deliberately and throws the ball at him, knocking Billy to the ground in the wet mud. Apparently, the film crew engaged a local fire engine to put hundreds, if not thousands of gallons of water onto the pitch, for just such an effect. Billy is plastered in mud. It was a cold day too, which didn't help matters. Although *Kes* was filmed during the school summer holidays, 1968 was remembered as a particularly cold and wet summer.

"Just look at this lot," says Billy to a classmate, showing him the sludge on his legs, arms, and shorts. Mr. Sugden barges through the players, scattering them like skittles, and when Tibbutt, the Tottenham Hotspur team captain protests, Sugden sends him off back to the changing rooms. Tibbutt is furious and sticks two fingers up at Mr. Sugden, adding, "The fat twat, 'e wants bleeding milkin', the big fat get."

"What did you say Tibbutt?"

"Now't sir"

One of Tibbutts teammates protests, "But he's our captain sir."

"I don't care who he is, we'll play this game like gentlemen, now get off back into the changing room."

Tibbutt wanders off the pitch, still seething.

As a matter of observation, I have seen many *Kes* tee-shirts, DVD covers and posters etc. showing Billy Casper using the two fingered salute, and it has since become such an iconic image that it is now commonly used and is basically representative of the *Kes* film. And yet, I cannot recollect a single scene in *Kes* where Billy himself raises his two fingers at anyone or at any time. Only Tibbutt performs this manoeuvre in *Kes* during the football match, or at least as far as I am aware, and I have viewed the film on countless occasions. Unless, of course, the films that I have viewed have all been abridged versions where certain scenes have been deleted. When *Kes* was first released, I knew that the posters, showing Billy with the famous two-fingered salute, which were pasted in prominent places in certain areas caused some offence because the message conveyed of course was 'Up Yours', or 'Screw You', and they were the polite versions. One manager of a local Yorkshire bus company simply refused to allow them to be displayed on any of his buses, but generally, everyone knew what they meant and accepted them with alacrity. Even Barry and Richard Hines's mother took offence at the huge poster that was set up in the village of Hoyland Common and said that she was afraid to show her face because of the rude connotations. Several still photographs were taken during the filming of *Kes*, possibly for media and advertising purposes and I believe that the Billy Casper two fingered salute could have resulted from one of these. I know of quite a few more of these film stills that exist, such as the one's featuring David 'Dai' Bradley, Barry and

Richard Hines and Tony Garnett, posing with two of the kestrels and others featuring Brian Glover and Colin Welland, all obviously stills taken during the 1968 film shoot and most seemingly in monochrome.

But I digress, back to the football match.

Soon Mr. Sugden, largely through brute force, equalises. The score now reads Tottenham Hotspur 1, Manchester United 1.

"And Bobby Charlton has equalised for Manchester United in this important fifth round cup tie at Old Trafford," blandly states a now happier Mr. Sugden.

The game now over, Billy gets into more trouble. He has no towel, so gets dressed quickly and tries to escape from the changing room before Sugden catches him, but he is too late. Mr. Sugden collars him as he is about to leave the changing room and asks Billy if he has had a shower and Billy, lying through his teeth, replies that he has had one, but Sugden doesn't believe him and asks the other lads if he has had a shower.

"Don't know sir," says Guthrie (Desmond Guthrie sadly died 2016). "Aven't seen him 'ave one."

Sugden asks the same question of the others, who all say, "'Aven't seen him have one sir."

Sugden turns to Billy, "That's because he hasn't had one, get in the shower Casper."

"I haven't got a towel sir," moans Billy.

"You can borrow one or drip dry. In the shower Casper."

"But sir."

"In the shower lad."

So, Billy strips off and enters the shower. Sugden places two lads at the shower entrance to ensure that he has a proper shower and doesn't come out until he has had one. Then Sugden, still smarting over Billy letting in the goal, turns the shower taps from hot to cold. Billy tries to get out of range of the freezing cold jets of water and even tries holding his hands over the spouts, to no avail. Eventually, Billy tries to climb naked over the shower wall. Tibbutt, spotting him and highly amused, shouts:

"Tuck 'em in Casper, tha privates are showin'."

My games teachers at school were just like Mr. Sugden. They were evil and masochistic against any lad that they didn't take to or who, like me, wasn't interested in sport. I know, I got the rough end on more than one occasion. They would chase us round the field and slap us hard on the buttocks with a plimsole, or even worse, a spiked running shoe. They were downright swines.

Mistakenly believing I had the shots of the real school safely in the can, it was time to search for the furthest target so far, namely the Cudworth Hotel, situated on the A628 and the site of the evening out for Billy's mum and her latest boyfriend and for Jud and his friends. Billy was left at home alone with two shillings on the mantlepiece for some pop and crisps, showing how uncaring she was for her youngest son. Billy wasn't too bothered though, for he had his new stolen falconry book to read. I knew through research that the Cudworth Hotel had once been managed by David Glover (no relation to Brian Glover), who played Billy's schoolmate Tibbutt. It had been renamed The Dard's since then but was sadly earmarked for demolition, according to the internet. The postcode that I put into the car's satnav took us to the right place sure enough, but the hotel was no longer there. It had already been demolished. I was in the right place for certain, for it had been situated on the corner of Sunningdale Drive, precisely where I was standing, but now only newly built houses stood in its place. Here I made another silly mistake, for I failed to photograph the houses that had replaced it. Stupidly, I simply forgot about my vow to photograph even indistinguishable sites and it niggled me for ages afterwards. I was halfway back down the M1 before I realised my error. That would now have to wait for another trip.

From here we headed back towards Hoyland Common, for the purpose of trying to locate Skiers Spring Colliery, which was used in *Kes* as Jud's place of work. From Hoyland Common, we took the A6135 for a mile or so until we reached Broad Carr Road on our left. From here, we drove along Broad Carr Road for almost a mile and then pulled into a layby. From this point, we could see a track that ran beneath an old iron bridge, and which ultimately led to the colliery, which now, of course, no longer exists, due to the closure of the mines that caused the miners's strike of 1984-85 and which destroyed most, if not all, of the close-knit mining communities in England [32]. Feelings ran especially high in the South Yorkshire coalfields area and many families were deeply affected by the strike, which they lost in the end due to the deindustrialisation policies of the Thatcherite government at the time. The area is now mostly secondary woodland and is another peaceful place to visit. I was struck by all the rural areas of Barnsley and its environs, which I was not expecting at all. I expected much more in the way of urbanisation, but so much of the area is green, open, and very pleasant. Having said that though, there is much recent development going on around Hoyland Common, more's the pity. So that was another site safely in the can.

We then headed back to Hoyland Common for lunch, where I took more images of Caspers Fish & Chips shop. We also had our wonderful fish and chip lunch there, well, it would have been rude not to, wouldn't it? We also renewed our friendship with Dave Rose. After lunch, we ventured along Fitzwilliam Street and secured some more useful images from the bottom of the street looking upwards [33]. The Hoyland Common Working Men's club was unfortunately closed yet again, but I noticed that the field opposite the bottom of the street appeared to be the same one where Jack Lee and I flew our kestrels back in 1968. Now though, there was a huge Hermes, now renamed EVRi, warehouse being constructed in blue and white materials just across the field. One thing is for sure, it certainly ruins the view for miles around, for it can also be seen from Tankersley churchyard.

We again paid our respects at Barry Hines's grave and took a few more pictures of it. Somebody had been since our last visit, for there were fresh flowers brightening up the scene. This time we had approached St. Peter's church at Tankersley by crossing back over the M1 and then, after a couple of hundred yards or so, we took a right turn into Westwood New Road and followed this road for several hundred yards, then took another left turn onto Black Lane and headed for the church on our left. At least, this route saved us from the long walk along Black Lane that we had endured on our last visit. As we were in the area, we decided to drive down Black Lane and re-visit Tankersley Old Hall. I love this place for it is so peaceful and I could not resist taking more photographs of this important site **[34]**.

Also, there were no leaves on the trees at this time of year so more of the ruin was in view for photography. This time, we walked into Bell Ground Wood for a short distance, taking more photographs, including some of a lovely clump of Jelly Ear Fungus *(Auricularia auricula judae)* which I found growing on a fallen elder branch. One day, as aforementioned, I planned to walk the full length of Bell Ground Wood, so named after the circular depressions caused by former open-cast mining operations. It was probably one of these depressions, filled with water, that Billy hurls a stick at in the film. The sun was beginning to sink towards the horizon, so as we had obtained all the shots on my list, we headed for home, where I began planning a third trip.

[26] Grange View, Blacker Hill, the site of the long since demolished coking plant where Billy Casper reads *The Dandy* comic. [27] Lewis Road where Billy Casper meets the milkman and steals a carton of eggs and a bottle of orange juice. [28] Looking up Lewis Road towards where the milk float was located. [29] The former betting shop where Billy Casper fails to place the bets on two horses for his elder brother, Jud. [30] St. Helen's Primary School, Monk Bretton. The buildings are similar in design to the secondary modern school at Athersley South that was used in *Kes* filming (that structure having been demolished some years ago). St. Helen's is the school attended by David 'Dai' Bradley real life, though in his time it was not on this site. [31] The modest grave of Brian Glover at Brompton Cemetery, London (courtesy of Ronnie Steele). [32] Site of the former Skiers Spring Colliery where Billy Casper's elder brother, Jud, worked. [33] Fitzwilliam Street, a road that Billy Casper walks up in *Kes*. [34] Tankersley Old Hall from the stile at the edge of Bell Ground Wood.

Chapter 4

The Barry Hines Memorial
(8th March 2022)

Again, I needed more images of more film locations, so I made a third shoot list which featured as follows:

1. The Alhambra Shopping Centre, Cheapside, Barnsley. In the film, Billy Casper walks by this centre with Kes on his glove (S70 1SB).

2. The Barry Hines Memorial, outside the Alhambra in Cheapside, Barnsley. Erected in Barry's memory by The Kes Group, which features a life size bronze sculpture of Billy Casper in a kneeling position holding Kes on his glove (S70 1SB).

3. The Yorkshire Bank, Market Hill, Barnsley. Where Billy, with Kes on his glove, talks to the elderly gentleman wearing a trilby hat (S70 2PL).

4. The Old Civic Hall, Barnsley. This is where the original library used to be situated in the film and from where Billy tries to unsuccessfully borrow a book on falconry (S70 2HZ).

5. Harrington Court, Lundwood. This is where the opening sequence shots for *Kes* were filmed (S71 5JR).

6. Site of the Cudworth Hotel, Cudworth, where Jud and Mrs. Casper had a night out, leaving Billy to read his falconry book (S72 8AG).

7. Tankersley Old Hall. Tankersley (S74 0DX).

8. Barry Hines's grave, Tankersley (S74 0DT).

Much of this shoot was centred on the town of Barnsley itself, which I had never been to before. There were several locations here that I needed to record for they played an integral part of *Kes*. There was also one object that I particularly wished to photograph, and that was the Barry Hines Memorial, situated directly outside the Alhambra Shopping Centre in the middle of the town. This bronze memorial was at the top of my shoot list for the day because it was in the form of a life-sized Billy Casper in a kneeling position with his kestrel on his glove. I had seen images of it on the internet, but I wanted to secure my own for the talk that I was putting together and for this book, which I had now begun to write.

So once again, David and I drove up the M1 motorway but, as we were going first to Barnsley, which is about five miles north of Hoyland Common, we came off at Junction 37. To achieve our goals, we had to use satnav, because we hadn't got a clue as to where we were going in Barnsley, although as the day progressed, we began to get to know Barnsley town centre rather well, or at least, parts of it! I knew that the statue was positioned on Cheapside, but that at first meant little to me as I had no idea where Cheapside was located, so, using the internet for the exact location, I tapped the postcode S70 1SB into the satnav which guided us into the Alhambra Shopping Centre. I had planned to park as close as possible to the Alhambra, but we couldn't have parked much closer if we tried, for we parked in the multi-story car park of the centre itself, which was a bonus, for I knew many of the film locations that I required were in a comparatively small area close to this spot. We eventually parked up, collected our ticket from the machine and set off on foot through the centre to find the statue. We were on the upper floor of the centre when I first spotted the statue, outside in the street below us, so we hurriedly made our way down the stairs to the ground floor and then outside to marvel at this iconic memorial [35]. Why we hurried I cannot recollect, for it was going nowhere, pure excitement I suppose. Cast in bronze, it was life-size and mounted on a columnar stone plinth. On one side of the plinth, set into the stone were the words in gold lettering [36]:

> THE
> BARRY
> HINES
> MEMORIAL

On the other side, in black lettering on a copper plate set into the stone, bore the inscription [37]:

> **BARRY HINES 1939-2016**
>
> Inspirational Author & Teacher
>
> Funds raised by the Kes Group:
> Ronnie Steele, Carl Yeates,
> Kris Branigan, Jan Brears,
> Janet Richardson & Milly Johnson.
>
> Funded entirely by private donations,
> With the support of
> Barnsley MBC.
>
> Sculptor: Graham Ibbeson M.A. (R.C.A.)

I had previously heard of author Milly Johnson from the Greg Davies film documentary *Looking for Kes*, and Graham Ibbeson had completed several such sculptures, including the one of the famous comedian Eric Morecambe in Morecombe Bay, Lancashire, which was unveiled by the Queen in 1999. The other names on the plaque I didn't know. In fact, I was completely unaware that a 'Kes Group' even existed. Had I known, I would have loved to have become involved in some way to help raise the funds for the memorial, perhaps give a free illustrated talk, but I was too late, these wonderful people had raised the £106,000 to pay for the statue, long before I had ever even heard of the venture. In fact, as previously stated, despite having an almost life-long obsession with the *Kes* story, it was Greg Davies's *Looking for Kes*, that rekindled the all-important spark. Besides, many of these wonderful functions were operated in Barnsley or its environs, so I never got to hear of them down in Nottingham, that is, not until I had begun my research much later.

Many people were posing with the memorial, as indeed did David and myself. David was particularly enamoured with the memorial as he is an excellent wood carver and plans to carve a smaller version of the statue in wood. I understand that smaller copies were made in bronze for £5,000 and some in resin for £1,500 and were all sold very quickly. They are highly prized possessions of the lucky people who purchased them, most of whom would not part with them at any price. These smaller copies helped enormously to raise the funds for the memorial statue. At the time of writing, I have yet to see one of these smaller replicas in the flesh, as it were, or indeed any of the commemorative mugs featuring an image of the statue and with the words 'Build it for Barry', emblazoned upon them and which were also created for sale, along with specially printed bags and badges to help with the funds. We spent some time with the statue, taking many photographs of it from various angles and of the Alhambra Shopping Centre itself, where in 1968, David 'Dai' Bradley as Billy Casper walked past here with Kes on his glove. Despite this, and the obvious fact that many more people would see the memorial here, I couldn't help but feel that Hoyland Common should also have a similar memorial in some prominent position within the village, I hoped that this would happen at some point in the future, it certainly needed to. During later research, I discovered that a new Billy Casper/Barry Hines statue was indeed on the cards for Hoyland Common. Apparently, once completed, it was planned to position it almost opposite Barry Hines's former house, number 78, on Hoyland Road in a small, lawned area. This statue apparently will not be made of bronze but matte black powder-coated steel. Perhaps this is a cheaper option than bronze. I discovered later that the Kes Group wished the Barnsley memorial statue to be placed in the centre of Barnsley marketplace, but the council would not sanction it. Still, it is in a good position in a busy part of the town and can easily be viewed by passers-by. In fact, if one is in the immediate environs, one can hardly miss it!

The next target on my list caused us no small problem and we wasted much valuable time. I desired to photograph the Yorkshire Bank at the bottom of Market Hill and the corner of Peel Square. This is where in the film, Billy talks about his kestrel to an elderly gentleman wearing a trilby hat outside the doors of the Yorkshire Bank. However, having abandoned the car, we now had to use our mobile phones for the postcodes, which I had written down on my shooting list. David logged in S70 2QE into his mobile phone and we set off to follow the displayed route. However, the route stated that the location was over a mile away towards the Doncaster Road, but the shot was important to me, and not knowing where we were going exactly, we had little choice. To cut a long story short, it transpired that the directions indicated on the phone, took us well out of the city centre and in the opposite direction from that we required, so when we finally reached our 'destination', I asked a passing couple if some houses across the road that the phone was telling us was indeed our destination, the former site of the Yorkshire Bank. They said they had lived there for many years and the only Yorkshire Bank they knew of was back in town. Brilliant! But we had already begun to suspect as much, so now we had no other choice than to retrace our steps back towards town. This miscalculation took well over a couple of hours out of our day, and I still had a long list to photograph. We must have somehow made a mistake with the postcode settings. If only we had taken the trouble to ask some of the locals in Barnsley, we would not have wasted so much valuable time. However, to be fair, we trusted the satnav of David's mobile phone, or at least, we trusted the accuracy of the postcodes we had logged in.

Once back in town, we headed back to the Barry Hines Memorial and from there, tried to plot the same route again. This time I also wanted to photograph the Old Civic Hall on Eldon Street, which was the original library used in *Kes*, but, yet again, the mobile phone played up and we ended up on Market Street. Here we asked a lady who was sat on a wall if she knew where the locations we were looking for were situated. She didn't really know but told us that the building in front of us was indeed at one time the Yorkshire Bank we were seeking. It was a similar-looking, corner positioned Co-Operative building, so I photographed it, even though I knew the stonework didn't look quite right. I wasn't wrong, for when I returned home, I checked it with an internet image of Billy Casper with Kes chatting to the man in the trilby hat, and it didn't match up. Thankfully, my images were digital, had they been film, I would have wasted many frames. Although I was unaware of it on the day, I discovered later that we had been a mere stone's throw from my objectives. In fact, at one point, we were only yards away. How annoying.

Because of the satnav error, time was now pressing, so I abandoned other locations in the town centre for another day and we returned to collect our car and headed out of Barnsley town centre for Priory Road in Lundwood, where we had previously photographed the betting shop and Lewis Road, where Billy met the milkman Duggie Brown. I took a second opportunity to photograph the milkman scene again on Lewis Road and preferred these later images to the former ones because the lighting was superior. This time though, my main goal in Lundwood was to find and photograph the opening scenes of the film, where the viewer looks down beyond the opening credits to view a steep, grassy hill, from where we see Billy Casper walking along the road below. This was filmed from the top of Harrington Court near where Priory Road meets Priory Place. However, when we arrived at the top of Harrington Court, past a row of garages, we were amazed to discover that the site was now completely unrecognisable from the same view in the film. An entire housing estate has now replaced the former grassy site. I drove down the hill to see if anything of the former site remained untouched, but it was just house after house all the way. Disappointed but undaunted, I drove back up the slope and photographed the site anyway, if only to show 'progress' **[38]**. Of all the sites that we had visited so far, this one was perhaps the most unrecognisable of all. Nothing remains forever I suppose. Feeling a trifle deflated, we moved further along the A628, out of Lundwood and on to the site of the Cudworth Hotel/Dards at Cudworth, the site of the public house where Mrs. Casper (Lynne Perrie) and Jud (Freddie Fletcher) had enjoyed their evening out. In the film, we are treated to the social evening at the Cudworth Hotel. The exterior of the Cudworth is not shown in the film, only the interior, where we see some banter from Jud against Reg (Joe Miller) Mrs. Casper's current boyfriend, who Jud seems to dislike. Jud then resumes chatting up the girls. The 4D Jones band provide the background music and the hilarious comedian Joey Kaye has a spot where he sings the popular double entendre *Marrow Song,* "Oh, what a beauty, I've never seen one as big as that before. Ooh what a whopper, it must be eighteen inches long or more," etc. etc.

We had returned to Cudworth to correct my former mistake of not photographing the site of the hotel. As previously stated, the Cudworth Hotel has now been demolished and I regretted not photographing the site on my last visit as it would have saved me from repeating the voyage. I was 99% certain that I was at the right place, on the corner of Sunningdale Drive, but just to make certain, I asked a local man walking his dog nearby and he confirmed it **[39]**. Several photographs were taken of the houses now occupying the site and we were then on our way back to Hoyland Common for, guess what? fish and chips at Caspers! This was becoming to be a habit, a very nice one though. This time, Dave Rose served me with a cod which matched the famous Billy Casper 'V' sign, which I duly photographed before consumption **[40]**. I now use the resulting image in my illustrated talk alongside an image of Billy Casper sporting his famous 'V' sign and it usually raises quite a few giggles. After lunch, I took photographs of Princess Street, including more, longer shots of Caspers showing its position on Princess Street, together with some views of the main road through Hoyland Common.

In the film and after the evening out at the Cudworth Hotel, Jud returns home drunk and wakes Billy up to help him get undressed and into bed, but Jud collapses on the bed, thus giving Billy the opportunity to get his own back.

"Tha drunken bastard, pig, sow, tha bastard, tha doesn't like being called a bastard, does tha, tha drunken bastard."

He slaps Jud across the face who then partly wakes up to shout at Billy, then collapses back into a drunken stupor onto the bed. Billy runs downstairs, hurriedly dresses, grabs his coat, and shoots out of the house into the early morning gloam before Jud can grab him. He then wends his way through Bell Ground Wood. This is one of my favourite parts of the film. It has such a peaceful and tranquil atmosphere here, especially with the early morning dappled sunlight filtering through the trees. It always reminds me of the woods that used to exist around my home and where many happy childhood hours were spent. Billy wanders along the woodland path, runs down a slope until he comes to the edge of the wood facing the old hall, where he watched the kestrels earlier. Having read some of his falconry book, Billy now feels a bit more confident to try and get his kestrel. Leaving the wood, he crosses the dirt track (Black Lane), climbs the low wall and heads across the field to the old hall, which as aforementioned is referred to as Monastery Farm in the film. Here, he climbs the vertical crumbling wall. David 'Dai' Bradley climbed this wall for real and a great job he made of it. Some pitons were placed into some of the more difficult parts of the ascent and some straw was placed below in case he fell, but nevertheless, he made the forty-foot climb unassisted. I can imagine the Health and Safety Executive sanctioning this today, I somehow think not!

The kestrel had been taken earlier by Richard Hines, but it had to be replaced in the eyrie for the scene to be shot. All credit to David 'Dai' Bradley for performing this manoeuvre. I have seen this wall for real and I certainly wouldn't fancy climbing it. Billy takes his young kestrel and returns home with his prize and from then onwards, his life begins to change for the better, or at least, for a while, for this is when Billy shakes off his 'jesses' from his constrained and deprived social life and becomes well and truly focussed and free from all the constraints of his home and the bullies and mind-numbing lessons at school, purely because of his newfound fascination with his young falcon. He feeds his kestrel, now named Kes, on sparrows that he 'shoots' in the garden and fields around his home. Of course, he doesn't really shoot them, the one that he is shown feeding to Kes was obtained by Richard Hines, possibly roadkill. Although the three kestrels were named 'Freeman, Hardy and Willis', after the well-known shoe company, Richard Hines named them after three inseparable miners who had become known affectionately by the same names. Even so, all three kestrels had to answer to the name Kes. As aforementioned all were covered legally by a government Home Office licence and this is very important. Perhaps a layman, unfamiliar with the art of falconry, could be forgiven for asking the question, 'Why did they need three kestrels?'.

This is a very good question, but as Richard Hines, or indeed any falconer would know, three kestrels would be the required minimum for this kind of work. To begin with, any more than three birds would have been very time-consuming regarding the training regime, so three would be ideal. To anyone but a discerning falconer, all three kestrels would be practically indistinguishable from each other, which is important, because perhaps only a falconer would notice any slight differences between them on film anyway. However, to an experienced falconer, there would be subtle differences in plumage markings and certainly in the character of the individual birds. This may come as a surprise to some, but just like humans, raptors, and indeed other birds possess individual traits in character, as in fact do most life forms. Some are easier to train than others, some are more docile than others, some are better flyers than others, some are chunkier, and others more rakish etc. But this still doesn't answer the question of; why three? The answer to this question is simple and concerns appetite and weight control. Falconers reward their birds when they return to the fist or lure, but these rewards soon take the edge off the bird's appetite. When this occurs, the bird loses its appetite and may then refuse to fly, or even worse, become disinterested in the proceedings and fly off, far and away over the furthest horizon and be at risk of becoming lost permanently. Additionally, some kestrels require more food than others, as in humans and most other life-forms. The filmmakers would require quite a lot of footage, so if only one kestrel was used, the time available for this would rapidly become exhausted. So, once one kestrel had been flown and rewarded a few times, its appetite would soon be satiated and it would thus become increasingly unsafe to fly and it would either refuse to perform further, or even fly away for good. Either way, it would therefore be unavailable for the cameras until the following day at least. Allowing for only one kestrel on set, the cameraman may easily not get enough of the required footage, so this is where kestrels number two and three come in. The first kestrel is returned to the mews for the remainder of the day but filming now need not be interrupted, for the remaining two kestrels are brought into play and filmed performing their aerial manoeuvres accordingly. This way, the film crew have optimised their time filming in the field by obtaining far more footage than would have been the case with only one bird. Of course, Richard Hines was well aware of this fact and acted accordingly, to his everlasting credit. Most people viewing the film would be completely unaware that three different kestrels were brought into play during the filming of *Kes* and all three, at some point, appear in the film.

Two of these kestrels came from the nearby Wentworth estate, but disaster struck early in the filming. Richard Hines unfortunately forgot to build a second door into the mews in Barry Hines's back garden, and this allowed Hardy to slip past him and escape. Kestrels can be very fast and can easily take one by surprise, as did this one. Filming had barely begun, and one kestrel had already been lost. It wasn't yet trained, so there was little chance of retrieving it, as proved to be the case. A second compartment and door would have prevented Hardy's loss because it would have been contained within this secondary compartment. Amazingly, Hardy was quickly replaced by the generosity of one of Richard's old school friends. If just Hardy had been the only bird used, filming these sequences would probably have had to have been put on hold for another year. Once all filming had finished, all three kestrels were safely hacked back to the wild. Hacking back to the wild is a process whereby the hawks are not just simply released and forgotten about. They are provided with food and placed in a familiar area where they are free to come and go as they choose. A careful watch is kept on this food supply until the hacked birds no longer return for it, having now becoming increasingly accustomed to fending for themselves in the wild and no longer require food to be left out for them. This is a common practice amongst falconers whom, once their young hawks are beginning to fend for themselves, instead of being allowed to continue, as the kestrels were in *Kes* after release, they are caught up and trained for falconry purposes in the time-honoured fashion. In the case of the kestrels used for *Kes*, once they were hacked back, they remained permanently in the wild to fulfil their natural lives, completely oblivious of their brush with fame.

Billy later mans (carries on the glove) Kes around the streets of Barnsley. Strangely enough, apparently, whilst filming, much to director Ken Loach's surprise, few people even noticed Kes sitting on Billy's gloved fist. Outside the Yorkshire Bank on Market Hill, an elderly gentleman eventually does ask Billy about Kes, and he tells the old timer that the bird is vicious and will fly at people. All nonsense of course, but entertaining. He walks past the Alhambra shopping centre on Cheapside, as well as other locations in the town centre of Barnsley.

Despite already having images of Tankersley Old Hall, I couldn't resist making another visit, basically because I needed some more images inside Bell Ground Wood and hopefully, more images of the hall from the opposing side behind the farmhouse, if possible. The track down to the old hall had become rather rutted to say the least, probably due to recent heavy rainfall, so it was fortunate that I was driving a four wheeled drive vehicle. I would have loved to have walked the full length of the wood, but due to our previous time wastage in Barnsley, darkness was not far away, so we only went in about fifty yards or so, but at least I secured some useful images. One day, I again vowed, I would have to return and walk the full length of this interesting looking wood. However, I did find a water-filled bell-shaped depression, possibly a remnant from the old opencast mining days and upon our return towards the old, rickety stile, I took images from inside the wood, facing the stile and with Tankersley Old Hall in the background, which is the exact view that Billy Casper would have had when viewing the kestrels flying in and out of the ruins [41 & 42]. There was just time enough to wander across to the farmhouse next to the ruins to ask permission to photograph the hall from a different perspective, but despite knocking on the farmhouse door, nobody answered, so I took three or four images from where I was standing by the farmhouse door. It was not what I really wanted, but I didn't wish to trespass on private property, so I left, and we then began the trip back up Black Lane to stop for a few minutes to pay our respects once more to Barry Hines's grave in St. Peter's churchyard. More flowers had been added to the grave and one of the ceramic birds had fallen from the tree and lay upside down on the grave, so we returned it to its original position on the tree. This concluded our third trip to the Barnsley region in my quest for film location images. However, because I had not found the locations in the centre of Barnsley, a fourth excursion was now deemed necessary.

[36]

[35]

THE BARRY HINES MEMORIAL

[37]

BARRY HINES 1939 - 201

Inspirational Author & Teacher

Funds raised by the Kes Group:
Ronnie Steele, Carl Yeates,
Kris Branigan, Jan Brears,
Janet Richardson & Milly Johnson.

Funded entirely by private donations,
with the support of
Barnsley MBC.

Sculptor: Graham Ibbeson M.A. (R.C.A.)

[38]

[39]

[40]

[35] The Barry Hines memorial outside the Alhambra shopping centre. [36 & 37] Inscriptions on the Barry Hines memorial. [38] Harrington Court, Lundwood, was used in the opening credits of *Kes* at which time it was a grassy field. [39] Site of what used to be the Cudworth (later Dard's Hotel). [40] A battered cod showing the famous Casper 'V' sign. [41] Possibly one of the former mining pits in Bell Ground Wood similar to the one in which Billy Casper threw a stick. [42] Tankersley Old Hall.

Chapter 5

Newsagents & Alleyways
(13th July 2022)

Although many of the *Kes* film locations were now safely recorded, there were several others that I simply had to find and photograph to complete my quest, particularly those in Barnsley town centre that had eluded us on our last visit. This time, I made doubly sure that I had the correct postcodes written down on my shoot list. This fourth shoot list reads as follows:

Barnsley Town Centre

1. The Yorkshire Bank on Market Hill, where Billy meets the elderly gentleman in the trilby hat (S70 2QE).

2. The Old Civic Hall, which housed the original library in 1968, Eldon Street (S70 2JR).

3. The site of the ABC Ritz cinema, Peel Street, where Kes was shown in Barnsley (S70 4DU).

4. The newsagent's shop, 23 Princess Street, where Billy had a paper round (S70 1PG).

5. Bridge Street, off Old Mill Lane, where Billy runs through an arch and picks up a cigarette packet, although I later discovered that this was not the correct location (S71 1PL).

6. Barnsley Chronicle, 47 Church Street, who often publish articles concerning *Kes*, thus helping to keep the memory alive and where Brian Glover once worked (S70 2AS).

Hoyland Common

7. Hoyland Common village sign.

8. 62 Tinker Lane, one of Barry Hines's former houses when younger (S74 0PW).

9. St. Peter's Church, Hoyland Common, opposite the field where Billy flies Kes, Hawshaw Lane-Law Hill (S74 0HH).

10. The field where Billy flies Kes (S74 0HH).

Tankersley

11. The corner of Bell Ground Wood, where David 'Dai' Bradley (Billy Casper) was photographed sitting on a fence, and the resulting image used for a *Kes* DVD cover (S74 0DX).

As before, my son David accompanied me on this fourth trip to Barnsley. Again, the weather was excellent, with bright sunshine and blue skies. If we could achieve all eleven images required for this shoot, this would render almost all the *Kes* film locations, or at least, those known to me so far to be complete. There are certainly other locations, but as yet, I had discovered no clues as to their whereabouts. It would certainly take another full day, so we set off at around eight in the morning for the M1 motorway. Just over an hour later, we were parked up at the Alhambra shopping mall in Barnsley town centre. Armed with my cameras and the shoot list, we bypassed the wonderful Barry Hines Memorial, where a young lady was singing through a microphone to all the passers-by. I already had enough images of the statue, so we walked further into the town centre where we headed for the Yorkshire Bank on Market Hill, which this time we found with ease [43]. It is no longer owned by the Yorkshire Bank, Virgin use it now, so we took photographs from various angles, so completing the first of the days shoot list. The bank of course is where Billy Casper meets the elderly gentleman wearing a trilby hat, who asks Billy about Kes. I felt that this was an important part of the story, not least because many of the locals didn't even notice the kestrel on Billy's fist during the film shoot. I have walked past members of the public with a Golden Eagle on my arm and they too didn't even notice. So, if they could miss a huge Golden Eagle, it is hardly surprising that they missed the comparatively diminutive Kes.

Not far from the bank and Market Hill is Eldon Street, the site of the library, where Billy is refused permission to take out a book on falconry. Knowing nothing about kestrels or falconry, Billy had taken the farmer's advice and travelled to town to visit the public library in search of a book on falconry. Here he is told by the librarian (Zoe Sunderland – born in 1944) that he cannot take out a book as he is not a member of the library. Replying that he only wanted to borrow a book on falconry, the librarian noticed Billy's filthy hands, so the following conversation went something like this:

"Well look at your hands, they're filthy. We'll end up with dirty books that way."

"A don't read dirty books."

"A should hope you don't read dirty books, ya not old enough to read dirty books."

The librarian shows Billy a document.

"Have you filled in one of these?"

"Don't know about that, only want to borrow a book on falconry. Me mam knows one of the people that works here tha know. That'll help wint it?"

"No, that doesn't help at all. You must still have the back signed. To be a member you must have someone over twenty-one who's on the borough electoral role to sign it for you."

"Aah well, am over twenty-one."

"You're not over twenty-one!"

"Aah but a vote."

"You don't vote, you're not old enough to vote."

"A do, a vote for me mam, she don't like votin' so a do it."

Billy was getting nowhere at the library, so he went off to find a bookshop. This is another part of the film that was based on Barry Hines's brother Richard, although unlike Billy, Richard Hines did not steal his falconry book. He ordered it from a bookshop but was informed it would be two weeks before delivery. This was too long, so, after ordering a copy, Richard returned to the library with a notepad and pencil and spent days copying large parts of the book in longhand, prior to the arrival of his own copy. Richard couldn't take the book out of the library as it was a reference book only and could not be removed from the premises. Our hero Billy though, had different ideas. He soon found what he was looking for, in a local second-hand bookshop, (which was filmed in Leeds, but the shop is now demolished) he checked to ensure no-one was looking, then slid the volume into his jacket and calmly walked out of the shop. This of course was in the days before security cameras. Like Billy Casper one of my earliest falconry books was interestingly the same edition that Billy stole from the bookshop, namely *A Manual of Falconry*, by Mike Woodford. In *Kes* it is referred to as *The Falconers Handbook*. The edition used in *Kes* was the same one of four editions that I still retain to this day in my library, this particular one featuring an adult goshawk on the dust jacket, the only difference being that, like Richard Hines, I didn't steal mine either.

Upon arrival home, Billy immediately begins to read his purloined book, but not for long, because his bullying older brother Jud snatches it from his grasp.

"Falconry, what's thou know about falconry," he growls.

"More than thee any road," snaps Billy.

"Falconry! Tha couldn't train a flea," yells Jud, keeping the book from Billy's reach.

"Where's tha goin' to get a Kestrel from then," gripes Jud.

"Am not tellin' thee," yells Billy.

Jud shoves Billy around, bends his arm and makes him tell Jud that he knows of the nest at Monastery Farm.

"Some other bird with less feathers is goin' to get lucky toneet," smirks Jud, as he throws the book back at Billy, and goes off to get himself ready for a night out at the Cudworth Hotel. Billy's mum also gets herself ready for a social evening, also at the Cudworth, leaving Billy home alone.

"There's two bob on the mantelpiece Billy, get yourself some pop and crisps for your tea," she instructs him, not really caring whether he does or not. Billy is too engrossed in his falconry book to even care about his neglect.

The site of the library still exists today and is not far from the bank. It is now the Old Civic Hall. This is a beautiful building and easily recognisable with its ornate façade [44 & 45]. We spotted it whilst some distance away and took several images from different angles. However, I wanted to go one step further, and try to obtain an interior shot of the ground floor room which had once housed the library. The entrance was open, so we ventured inside, where we spoke to a lovely security guard who was most helpful, although he didn't know which of the rooms had formed the old library as he had only been working there for a few months. However, he did inform us that it was now being used as a facility for young offenders. He asked a lady member of staff if we could try to locate and photograph the room and she kindly obliged. She showed us into several rooms, all on the ground floor, but only one of them would have been of a size big enough for a library, so I photographed that. I was happy enough with this [46]. Thanking them both, we then left the building to concentrate on the third item on my list.

This was the former site of the ABC cinema which was one of the first Yorkshire towns to show *Kes* after its official World Premiere at the ABC cinema in Doncaster. And quite right too. I knew the Ritz had been demolished but I also knew that it had been situated on Peel Street, which we soon found. However, after walking up and down Peel Street a couple of times, it became obvious that we weren't going to find the exact location without some help from the locals, all of whom were most obliging. The younger one's didn't really know, which was understandable, they wouldn't have been born then, or learnt about it at school, so we concentrated our enquiries with the more elderly inhabitants, several of whom were able to inform us with much conviction, that if we walked up Peel Street on the left-hand side of the road towards the top, we would come to the Lidl supermarket, and that was the site of the former Ritz cinema, and so it proved to be. Again, more images were taken of the Lidl supermarket. Three items on our shoot list had already been attained within barely an hour of our arrival in Barnsley. We couldn't believe our luck and it was a vast improvement compared to our last visit.

I wanted to find a bookstore where I could perhaps buy an A-Z street plan of Barnsley town centre to help us find the street locations more easily and David spotted The Book Vault bookshop at 7 Market Street. So, we ventured inside. The proprietor had no A-Z's but did find me an ordnance survey map of the Sheffield, Barnsley, and Rotherham areas, so I purchased that. Before leaving however, the shop owner showed me a copy of the book *Build it for Barry*, by Ronnie Steele, a copy of which I had been seeking for quite some time. This book contains much valuable information for *Kes* enthusiasts, because the author had been taught at school by none other than Barry Hines himself and Brian Glover, who was also a teacher. Ronnie is also part of the Kes Group which helped to raise the funds for the Barry Hines Memorial statue. I didn't realise it until I arrived home with my copy of the book that it was also signed by Ronnie. So that was a bonus. The Book Vault bookshop had also helped the Kes Group with their *Build it for Barry* project.

Feeling very pleased with my two purchases, it was time to set off for the fourth location on my list. This was the newsagents, for whom Billy Casper worked as a newspaper delivery boy and where he also stole chocolate bars and suchlike, the rogue. I really needed to find this location, but all I knew for certain was that it was on Princess Street. I thought it coincidental that two of the locations for *Kes* were on two different Princess Streets in two different areas, namely, this one in Barnsley and the other, Caspers Fish & Chips shop in Hoyland Common a few miles away to the south. This Princess Street was a bit more difficult to find and was further out from the city centre. In fact, we were nearer to it when we were at the Lidl supermarket, so we had to retrace our steps and follow the postcode in David's mobile phone. We also asked an elderly lady where Princess Street was located and why we wished to find it. She was most helpful and said that as she was going that way anyway, she would take us there, and so she did, no doubt saving us quite some time. Princess Street was made up of mostly terraced houses whose front doors opened directly onto the pavement, and the old newsagents was no different. We soon found it on the right-hand side of the street at No. 23, although now it is a private dwelling **[47]**. I knew what the building looked like for I had seen a recent image of it on the internet. When Billy arrives late to take his paper round, due to Jud nicking his bike, the newsagent warns him that there are plenty of other, more trustworthy kids who would be glad of Billy's job, especially those on the new estate, but Billy tells him:

"I 'aven't let thee down yet, 'ave I?" whilst stealing a bar of chocolate behind the newsagent's back.

"That's because I haven't given you the chance," smugly utters the newsagent, not realising that Billy has been pilfering from him for ages.

David took some images of me standing beside the building and I took several more. The windows had changed since *Kes* was shot here and their original window positions could still be determined in the brickwork. I was really pleased that we had found this location for it featured strongly in the film by demonstrating some of Billy's character early on. It was beginning to amaze me how Ken Loach, the director, and Tony Garnett, the producer, had discovered all these locations. A gentleman living across from this house remembered it being used for the film and was very interested in what we were trying to do. We chatted with him for quite some time, and he told us that he remembered the film crew's presence there. Like many other people we spoke to in Barnsley, *Kes* was his all-time favourite film too.

The next location took us right across the other side of the town centre and was the longest walk on this trip. We were beginning to feel the heat of the day by this time, for it was the beginning of the 2022 heatwave and all the walks up and down the sloping streets were beginning to have an affect. We walked past the magnificent town hall building and photographed it, if only because the Barnsley council, housed within its offices, have done next to nothing to capitalise on this famous film. So much could have been achieved if the right people were in charge, but as is so often the case, it is the wrong people who have all the power. It was left to private individuals, such as those within the Kes Group, to arrange and pay for the Barry Hines Memorial and the blue commemorative plaque in Hoyland Common. We walked on past the town hall and more by accident than design, we came across another building on my shoot list, that of the Barnsley Chronicle at 47 Church Street **[48]**. I photographed this building because they have often published articles concerning *Kes*, thus helping to keep alive its perpetual memory. Not only that, but Brian Glover began his working career here in the advertising department. So, with that connection firmly in mind, we ventured inside to ask if we were still on the right track for our final shoot in Barnsley for the day. The young lady receptionist was most helpful and gave us directions for Old Mill Lane, which was not far away, and Bridge Street, which was our goal. We wandered down Old Mill Lane and underneath a railway bridge until we came to Bridge Street on our right. Here I needed to find the archway that Billy Casper runs through and out of the far side. The camera had remained fixed on the spot to film Billy return quickly, pick up a discarded cigarette packet, look through it, just in case he might find something of interest concealed within, then, disgusted that it was empty, throws it away and disappears again. We walked the full length of Bridge Street, but no archways were present. This was odd, because I almost knew for certain that they remained, so I said to David that we should retrace our steps and check to see if Bridge Street continued across Old Mill Lane on the far side, as is sometimes the case. Whilst retracing our steps, we noticed a black Mercedes car bearing the number plate KA13 PER (Casper) **[49]**. This was amazing and I couldn't resist taking a picture. David also spotted another car with a similar 'Casper' number plate as we were leaving Barnsley. This amply still demonstrates the popularity of *Kes* in the Barnsley area even after its making over half a century ago. Some people have even had their vehicles sprayed with Casper and *Kes* images whilst others carry similar tattoos on their torso's. There is at least one instance of a local couple who named their child Kes after the film. I discovered the latter from a newspaper article which is held in the Barry Hines Archive in the Special Collections Department at Sheffield University, which I was to visit later in 2023.

Crossing back over Old Mill Lane, we soon discovered that Bridge Street did indeed continue and that there was not one archway between the houses, but four! I photographed all four, just to be certain that I had the right one, but I believed at the time that the one furthest along the street was the right one because the slope behind it was steeper than the others, although newer houses had since been built on the slope below **[50]**. I also remembered from the film that Billy ran around the corner and straight through the first archway. So, this was the archway that I concentrated my efforts upon. Railed gates had also been erected in front of the arch, so I poked my lens through these to obtain the closer view that I required. I later confirmed that this was the correct archway, or at least, I thought I did, (more about this later) because I viewed the film again at this point and we see Billy, running round the corner and straight into and through this arch. Ever since, I have referred to this archway as 'Fag Packet Alley'. Again, I made another error. I failed to photograph the corner of the road where Billy runs towards the arch. This would have to now be rectified at a future date. This completed all the shots that were on my list for Barnsley Town centre, so we made our way back to the car, ready for the drive down to Hoyland Common. However, a recent April 2023 conversation with Ronnie Steele threw a spanner in the works regarding the actual location for 'Fag Packet Alley'. Ronnie informed me that Bridge Street and the alley on this street was not the *Kes* film location I believed it to be. The true location was one parallel street lower down called Honeywell Street, which overlooked the Star paper mill, and which was demolished during the 1970s. This of course now meant another visit to photograph this area during a future trip.

*****

I needed to return to Hoyland Common to secure images of three more locations, but also, we were by now really looking forward to a slap-up meal of fish and chips at Dave Rose's beloved Caspers Fish & Chips shop on Princess Street. However, this time we were to be bitterly disappointed, for the shop was closed. Was it due to the hot weather? Was Dave on holiday, or had he already sold the business? I wasn't sure. Dave had informed us on our last visit that he had planned to retire by September of 2022 and was about to advertise it for sale. This was a minor disaster, but we decided to carry on with securing the images before we went off elsewhere in search of some sustenance.

The first item that I needed to photograph was the village road-sign, which was easily obtained. I required this more for the illustrated talk that I was compiling, rather than anything else. With this accomplished, it was then off down Hoyland Road to Tinker Lane, which has the Star public house on the left-hand corner. We drove down Tinker Lane for a short way until we came to No. 62 **[51]**. This, according to the archives at Sheffield University, is one of the dwellings where Barry Hines lived during his formative years. The property consisted, to my surprise, of two small semi-detached bungalows. The brickwork seemed rather modern, so we wondered if the original building had been demolished and replaced with these two tiny bungalows. Either way, I photographed the site for posterity, if nothing else. By this time, I had become interested in discovering the former houses that Barry Hines had lived in, for these were tangible memories of the author that I could record photographically, that is of course, if I could discover their whereabouts. Through my research, I was to shortly discover several of the latter.

The next location was very important to me. I was aware that there were other fields that had been used during filming, but this one was the main field where all the kestrels were trained by Richard Hines and were also flown there by David 'Dai' Bradley. This was an important part of *Kes*, for, as Jarvis Cocker stated in *Looking for Kes*, this is where Billy shakes off his troubled home and school life and becomes elated with Kes's performance in the air. For a while, he is at peace with the world. I thought we had located this field on one of the recent visits to Hoyland Common, but as I later suspected, I had the wrong location, so I renewed my research and came up with the correct one. We drove east a short way along Hoyland Road until we came to Hawshaw Lane and with St. Peter's Church on our right (not the same St. Peter's church where Barry Hines is buried at Tankersley) and parked the car in a wide lay-by just up the road. I had noticed a footpath beside a cemetery on the opposite side of the road from the church, so we ventured along it. It was rather narrow, and I wondered how the film crew had managed to transport all their equipment along this narrow trail. We progressed for about one hundred yards or so and took a left turn into the cemetery. Here we spotted a nearby large squarish tower known as Lowe Stand on our right. It is an 18th century folly, built possibly as a hunting lodge for the 1st Marquess of Rockingham and is now a grade two listed building. I only mention this because by a remarkable coincidence, during our visit, a male kestrel was perched atop the tall tower. Then a thought struck me. Was this male kestrel a descendent of one of those that had been used during the making of *Kes*? After all, they had all been hacked back into the wild somewhere in the vicinity, had they not? Therefore, it is not beyond the realms of possibility that the bird perched on Lowe Stand could quite easily have been a descendant of one of the three famous kestrels used in the film. I would like to think so. I had seen many images of this tower during my research, including a painting of it on the wall of Caspers Fish & Chips shop, but until now, I had never seen it for real. Making our way through the cemetery, we came across a much wider track leading to the main flying field. It now became obvious to me that this must have been the track that the film crew would have used. This large field is now a sports field but to my pleasant surprise, it looks little different from when *Kes* was filmed here in 1968. We walked down the same short slope into the field that Colin Welland ventured along when, as Mr. Farthing, he went to watch Billy fly Kes **[52]**. It was an amazing experience to be on this same field and I asked David to photograph me here, with my arm outstretched, calling, "Here Kes, come on girl." This completed all but one of the shots on my list, and it all had taken little over three hours.

*****

One final shot remained. I had a photograph of Billy Casper sat on a fence with Kes and which was used as a cover image for a foreign issue of a *Kes* DVD. I was 99% sure that I knew where this photograph had been taken. It was at the lower corner of Bell Ground Wood, opposite Tankersley Old Hall, from where Kes was taken for the film. It was only a short drive from Hoyland Common to Tankersley and down Black Lane to the old hall. Here we parked up and as I had the DVD image on my mobile phone, I compared it with the scene before me. I was right, even after 54 years, the woods on the horizon proved beyond doubt that this was indeed the scene, so we secured several images here **[53]**. I resisted the temptation to take more of the old hall itself because, not only did I already have enough, but with it being high summer, the view was partly obscured by the surrounding trees in full leaf. Thus, at least for now, I had secured all the actual film locations for *Kes* that were known to me. The book shop scene where Billy steals *A Manual of Falconry* by Mike Woodford, was filmed in Leeds, but as the shop has long since been demolished, it seemed rather pointless going all the way to Leeds just for this one shot, the location of which we might not even discover.

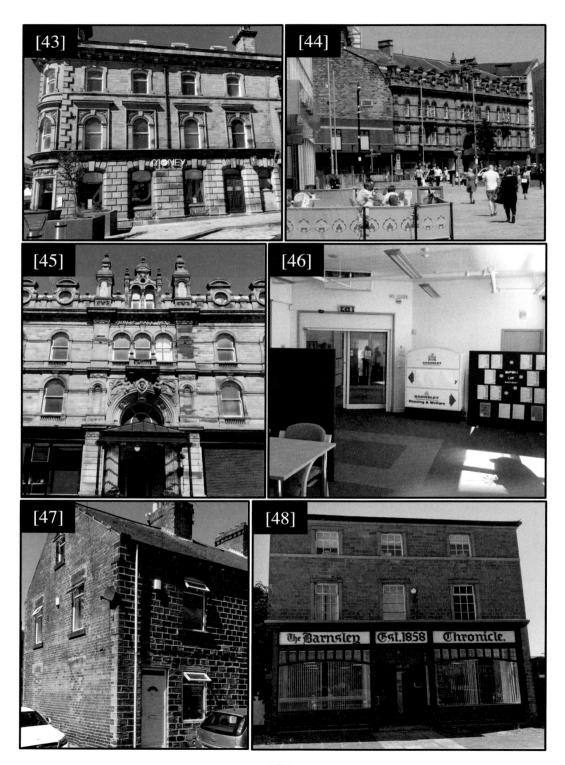

[49]

[50]

[51]

[43] It was outside this former Yorkshire Bank in Market Hill that Billy Casper meets the elderly gentleman wearing a trilby hat who engages Billy with questions about Kes. [44 & 45] Barnsley Public Hall (now Barnsley Civic Hall) in Eldon Street which once housed the public library where Billy Casper attempts to borrow a falconry book. [46] Interior of what would have been the library. [47] The former newsagents in Princess Street where Billy Casper had his paper round. [48] Offices of the *Barnsley Chronicle* in Church Street. [49] Maybe a coincidence but this car number plate would be appropriate for any *Kes* fan. [50] 'Fag packet alley' in Bridge Street is very similar to the one used in *Kes* when filming took place in 1968. [51] Barry Hine's former home in Tinker Lane. [52] Entrance to the field where Billy Casper is seen to fly Kes. [53] The corner of Bell Ground Wood where David 'Dai' Bradley was photographed sitting on a fence for the *Kes* DVD cover.

Chapter 6

Bell Ground Wood
(14th October 2022)

There were still a few loose ends that required tidying up, so a fifth trip was now on the cards. As usual, I wrote out a shoot list, although the requirements for this visit were somewhat less than on previous occasions. The list reads as follows.

Tankersley

1. Bell Ground Wood. Ever since beginning this quest, I had long desired to walk the full length of the woods where Billy Casper had trodden on his way to take Kes from the ruins of the old hall. This had now become a priority.

Hoyland Common

2. Caspers Fish & Chips shop. I needed to discover if Dave Rose had indeed sold the chip shop and whether the new owners, if any, had changed its name and décor, or if, it had been demolished. I sincerely hoped not.

Barnsley

3. The Yorkshire Bank where Billy Casper chats with the elderly gentleman in the trilby hat. I had done this before but for some reason had basically excluded the section where the actual conversation had taken place.

4. The Book Vault shop on Market Street to photograph the exterior and to purchase another copy of *A Kestrel for a Knave* (S70 1SL).

5. The Barnsley Antiques Centre, where items produced to raise funds for the Barry Hines Memorial were offered for sale. Situated in The Basement, 16 Doncaster Road, Barnsley (S70 1TH).

As on my last four photoshoots in and around Barnsley, my son David accompanied me yet again. He must be a sucker for punishment! It was good to be visiting 'Kes Country' again. The first change on our route up the M1 was a change of direction. We came off at junction 36 as usual, but this time, instead of heading east towards Hoyland Common, we headed west on the A61 for a short distance before turning off to the right and down Westwood New Road, heading for Black Lane on our left and St. Peter's church at Tankersley. From the church, we journeyed down to Bell Ground Wood, where I planned to walk the full length of the wood for the first time. I had wanted to do this ever since our first trip in 2021, but since our first trip in 2021, but there was never enough time due to the busy shooting schedules. This time, I kept the shooting schedule small enough to allow for a more leisurely day. I took a few more images of Tankersley Old Hall, well, I couldn't resist it, and then we turned into Bell Ground Wood. Previously, we had only ventured a few yards into the wood and that was never enough for me. I hoped to tread where Billy Casper had trod, if any of the wood was still recognisable after more than half a century that is. I began immediately to take photographs, not just of the wood and tracks throughout, but also some of the vegetation. As a lifelong naturalist, I wanted to discover, as far as possible, and in the time available, some of the flora and fauna that existed in the wood. Of course, to obtain a real idea of the wildlife in the wood, I would need many visits over several months, including the use of a mercury vapour moth trap, so I could only, at best, acquire a fleeting glimpse of the wild occupants of the wood. But that would be better than nothing.

Bell Ground Wood is a fairly large mixed deciduous woodland, containing a fair number of magnificent high forest beech trees along with silver birches, common elm, sycamore, horse chestnut, large-leaved lime, and oak, with an understorey of many saplings of all these species, together with holly, hazel, ivy, and a further ground cover of bramble which continuously wrapped around our feet. Even a hornbeam had been planted close to where we accessed the wood, with the plant nursery labels still attached. There were several hawkweeds still in flower and a solitary spike of the broad-leaved helleborine orchid, which of course, with this being October, was well past its flowering period, but was still easily recognisable. On one of the large-leaved lime trees in the wood, we found many nail gall tubes standing some 8mm and erect from the leaves, resembling little spikes. These are caused by a tiny mite which over-winters on the trunk of the tree.

By the side of the main pathway, we presently came upon the remains of a wood pigeon. Well, to be more accurate, it consisted of merely a few dozen plucked feathers. These had all the hallmarks of a raptor kill, most likely that of a female sparrowhawk or possibly a goshawk. The goshawk has made a remarkable comeback to the British Isles after being extinct here for many decades, mostly through lost falconers's birds. Either way, it was certainly a raptor that killed the pigeon, for the feathers were obviously plucked and not chewed out as they would have been had a four-footed predator, such as a fox done the deed. Close beside the wood pigeon kill, was a narrow dyke which ran beneath the pathway. Growing in the natural walls of this dyke were two fern species, namely, the hart's tongue fern and the lady fern. A colourful splash of red against all this green came in the form of rosehips adorning the trailing stems of the wild dog rose. Due to the drought, there was no water in the dyke, although the surrounding woodland floor appeared damp enough.

As we started along the main pathway, the harsh shriek of a jay shattered the silence of this lovely wood. This beautiful member of the crow family, however, remained hidden from view. As did a pair of common buzzards, whose plaintive mewing's could be heard above the tree canopy, but like the jay, remained out of sight. One cast its lethal shadowy form on the sun dappled ground from above, through gaps in the tree canopy. Grey squirrels were present in some force, due to the huge quantity of beech mast which littered much of the woodland floor. We presently came to a crossroads, where a path crossed our front. Some of this woodland was fenced off with strands of barbed wire. We took a left turn and soon discovered the reason for the barbed wire. We approached an open five-barred gate, upon which sported a signboard, stating that this part of the wood was private property and belonged to the Wentworth Estate. Those words rang a bell in my mind. Where had I heard of the Wentworth Estate? Then it all came flooding back to me. Of course, Wentworth Estate was the estate that had supplied two of the kestrels for *Kes*. Not wishing to trespass in this part of the wood, we turned around and headed back down the trail until we came to another left fork, which was outside the barbed wire fencing. The path here was quite wide, several feet or so, and we decided to follow it to its conclusion. I was taking scores of images along the way, searching for likely areas that could have been included in *Kes*, but to be truthful, this was difficult as I had to try and remember Billy Casper's walks through the wood from memory of my numerous viewings of the film, but obviously, over fifty years of continuously growing vegetation which must have blotted out much of the original landscape.

We found several of the bell-shaped pits from the previous mining excavations and photographed all of these as we came across them, although most of these were inundated and overgrown with vegetation of one sort or another. A late speckled wood butterfly flitted haphazardly in the sunshine before disappearing further along the track. After about half an hour, we spotted the far end of the wood, which was marked by a wooden stile, which I have to say, was in much better condition than the rickety old thing we had crossed upon our entering the wood **[54]**. Here I again made a mistake, which yet again I didn't realise until back at home in Nottingham. I should have crossed this stile into the fields beyond because I felt almost certain that the scene where Billy Casper runs towards the wood from nearby Hoyland Common while searching for Kes at the end of the film, was at this end of Bell Ground Wood. Open fields were visible from beyond the stile and as such, I feel fairly certain that this could be the field in front of the wood where Billy climbs a five-barred gate, swinging his lure during his search for the missing Kes. This oversight gave me another reason to return to Bell Ground Wood, not that another reason was needed mind you. The opening of the wood at this stile allowed a wonderful halo of light to enter and which penetrated some distance into the wood, illuminating plants and trees with its warm glow.

Unlike 54 years ago though, the huge EVRi warehouse had now spread right to the very edge of Bell Ground Wood. It loomed large atop a steep slope to our left. I hope it progresses no further, unlike much of the developments around Hoyland Common. I had seen this development on previous occasions and had read complaints about it on the internet from the locals and with good reason, for new roads with their accompanying large islands, together with new housing estates and warehouses has desolated much of the surrounding land. Huge plots of land have been bulldozed to oblivion, destroying all wildlife that once abounded there. Barry Hines would not have been happy, I am sure.

I photographed the stile from inside the tree canopy to capture the glow of light emanating from beyond the stile and then headed deeper into the wood, venturing off the path at several intervals, finding more of the bell-shaped pits, which in some cases were almost completely overgrown with vegetation. None contained water due to the lack of any recent rain. I attempted to find the slope that Billy ran down and I am almost sure that I found it, or at least, one very much like it. I photographed it any way. We then came across a large beech tree which had some initials carved upon its massive greyish trunk. The initials were dated 1960. I was still at school in 1960 and as such, I paused for a moment's thought. Was the person who carved these initials still alive? I hoped so. The tree was obviously large in 1960 but its girth had grown considerably in the sixty-two years that had since elapsed, and as such, the initials had stretched due to the enlargement of the bark around the trunk through subsequent growth and most of the lettering was now largely illegible, apart from the 1960 date, which was still just about decipherable [55]. I also reflected that these initials would have been on this tree when David 'Dai' Bradley as Billy Casper, passed this way in 1968 during the making of *Kes*. I wondered if he, or any of the film crew had ever noticed them? They would have been rather more decipherable back then.

Much to my surprise, fungi were almost non-existent, but I put this down to the long, hot, and dry summer of 2022. As aforementioned, there had been very little rainfall for weeks on end, which is not generally conducive to good fungal growth. I found three or four very small clumps of sulphur tuft growing on some old tree stumps and a single pleated inkcap, but that was all. We had obviously arrived at an unfortunate season for fungi in this wood because I am sure that in normal years, there would have been many species present due to the mixture of deciduous tree species. The woodland floor was damp enough when we were there, but probably not for long enough.

Photography completed; we were loathe to leave this charming wood. There hadn't been a breath of wind all morning. The bright sunlight was filtering through the tree canopy as leaves were falling earthwards and carpeting the ground, heralding that autumn was well on its way. It was so peaceful and not a single human in sight, but I needed to find out what was happening at Caspers Fish & Chips shop and then to drive up to Barnsley to complete the day's shoot. Even so, we called in at St. Peter's churchyard as usual on our way back up Black Lane to pay our respects to Barry Hines at his graveside. This was now becoming a regular occurrence, but I simply could not bypass this lovely churchyard and not visit, it just didn't seem right. Yet again, someone had been since we were last there in July and had placed fresh flowers on the grave.

Part of the road after Black Lane was now open again. It had been closed since our very first visit over a year previously, so we took this route which saved us going back the way we had come from the M1. However, this new section did not bring us out immediately opposite Hoyland Road as I had expected. New roads had been constructed and I missed a turning, so had to drive to the next island and turn back to find the road to Hoyland Common on our right. At least, this brought us out onto Sheffield Road, from where it was a short drive past Fitzwilliam Street and to take a right turn at the crossroads onto Hoyland Road. We could see the sign for Caspers Fish & Chips shop as we passed the Star public house, and a short drive took us to Princess Street and on to Caspers. The shop was still closed, and it looked as though it had been closed since our last visit in July. At least, all the external original Caspers signage was still in place, but for how much longer I wondered? Whether all the signed photographs were still inside, I had yet to discover. It would be a crying shame if any new owners removed all traces of the *Kes* film from the premises. We asked a passing lady if she knew what was happening to the shop, but she had no idea, as she was only visiting her daughter. We didn't even get out of the car. What was the point? (I later discovered from the internet that it appears that the shop is now permanently closed.) How sad. I am so grateful that we visited before the axe finally fell. However, we used the opportunity to drive the full length of Tinker Lane beside the Star, which turned out to be a dead-end. This is the lane where Barry and Richard Hines once lived. I took the opportunity to take a couple of extra images of No. 62 Tinker Lane from a slightly different angle to my previous attempt, and then it was off to Barnsley to complete the day's shoot.

Instead of re-joining the M1 and heading north for junction 37, I decided to go by the back road through Birdwell, which was a straight enough run and after a few miles, brought us into the town of Barnsley. We were getting to know our way round now. Even so, I had written down the postcodes just in case we needed to use the satnav, but we didn't need them at all, for we soon found ourselves parking at the Alhambra Shopping Centre again. We bypassed the Barry Hines memorial on foot and headed for my first target, the old Yorkshire Bank on Market Hill. I had photographed this building before, but basically from the wrong side. Billy Casper had spoken to the elderly man in the trilby hat on the Peel Square side and I hadn't quite obtained the right angle on our last visit. I planned to put this right. There are two ATM's there now, which obviously didn't exist in 1968, but the place was still identifiable. There was a lot of people about, some of them using the ATM's but I took the shots anyway. I knew this was the right place due to the stonework and had taken a screengrab on my phone just to be certain we were at the exact spot. The stonework was different here from the rest of the building, and this is readily identifiable in the original film footage.

The next target on my list was The Book Vault shop at 7 Market Street, which was situated just off Peel Square [56]. I took three or four images of the shop frontage before venturing inside to ask the owners if they minded me using the images for this work and my *Kes* talk. Fortunately, they had no objection to this and gave me permission. Obtaining copies of *A Kestrel for a Knave* are not as easy to come across as one might imagine, especially where second-hand bookshops and charity shops are concerned. Despite constant searching for several years, I have yet to see a single copy of this book in any charity shop anywhere, despite the countless thousands of copies that have been printed in many editions and languages since 1968. Owners of this work must surely be hanging on to them. However, copies are usually available on eBay or Amazon. I knew The Book Vault, however, did stock it as I saw a couple of copies on my previous visit and so I purchased two copies on the spot, one for myself and one for my son. These were of the paperback edition printed in the year 2000, and was the same edition that Greg Davies took with him when he was filming *Looking for Kes*. So now I had three different editions of the book in my library. The Book Vault had also hosted signing sessions for many authors including Ronnie Steele with his *Build it for Barry* book, which, of course, is how I obtained my signed copy on a previous visit.

The Barnsley Antiques Centre had also stocked *Build it for Barry* items and I hoped to acquire a mug, T-shirt, or a badge from this shop, which we had bypassed when we went on our previous mis-guided search for filming locations. So, I knew where to find this shop and set off after lunch in a café which we found on Albert Street. We soon found the antiques centre as it was only a short stroll from the Alhambra Shopping Centre, and it was an amazing place. It was crammed with all manner of items, from militaria, stuffed birds, jewellery, furniture, books and DVD's, witchcraft items, and countless other curios in several rooms, rented by several different dealers. We spent quite some time in here, marvelling at all the artifacts before I asked about the *Kes* memorabilia. Unfortunately, whoever owned the *Build it for Barry*, stock had collected it some eighteen months prior to our visit as it was required for a *Kes* exhibition elsewhere. There had not been much of it left anyway apparently, so I was a bit disappointed. This concluded the day's shoot and so we made our way back to the M1 and home. Perhaps not surprisingly, because of my visits to Barnsley and Hoyland Common, plus all the intermediate research and speaking with the locals and writing the Barnsley dialect from *Kes* for this book, I found myself beginning to speak with a slight Barnsley accent, tha knows!

But there was still one more venue that I particularly wished to visit, and this was the Barry Hines Archive in the Special Collections Department at Sheffield University. This would, of course, necessitate a 6th photographic shoot, if possible. In the meantime, I was desirous of adding a few screenshots from the original film, particularly those that showed identifiable background scenery so that I could compare it with my images taken 55 years later. However, to simply take screenshots and publish them in my book could land me in hot water for using them without prior copyright permission. This would certainly constitute a copyright infringement, and this would never do; I would much rather not use them at all and instead rely entirely on my own self-taken images. However, it was worth a try and to this end, I wrote to Windfall Films who had, along with Ken Loach's Kestrel Films, made the classic film in the first place. I received a rapid reply from Steven Hess who informed me that Windfall Films had recently and sadly been dissolved. Steven very kindly informed me that MGM now held the copyright, and he gave me their contact e-mail. For some now forgotten reason, I had previously believed that Sony had held the copyright, which no doubt explained why I had heard nothing from Sony when I requested screenshot copyright of *Kes* from their offices. Needless to say, I lost no time in writing to MGM by email.

The very next day, I received the reply from Clipstill. MGM's Senior Coordinator for Media Licensing and Advertising manager, Shannon Muchow, who was very receptive. This was a very interesting email which confirmed that MGM did indeed hold the copyright for *Kes*. Shannon required a bit more information from me and listed six points.

1. Title of book.
2. Do you have the still images from the film, and could I share with what images I could compare them.
3. Expected first print run.
4. Territory (UK only, Worldwide, etc.).
5. Expected Publishing Date.
6. Complete Licensee Information (address, phone, e-mail etc.).

It transpired that the usual license fee was $100.00 per interior image and $2,000 for a front cover. These fees did not include in context advert promotions, which would result in a matching fee. Once I sent this information, which I did almost immediately, my request would be submitted for an internal review.

At least, I now had a good idea of the requirements needed, so I replied, stating that I did not yet have a publisher, which at this juncture, was true enough. Once I had found a publisher, I would renew contact again. Shannon replied stating that she would check with their archives to discover any photographs that they held and would get back to me.

Shannon then very kindly sent me a much more detailed email, where I was very surprised to discover that MGM had been recently acquired by Amazon, which, as she stated, may change the future situation somewhat. She also said that she had reached out to another author who had recently licensed a still image of Billy Casper reading the *Dandy* comic in front of the clanking, smoke billowing coking plant. I wondered who this could have been? Apparently, Shannon asked them as to where they acquired this image as she had no access to this in their archives. I knew that there were many screenshots of *Kes* on the internet, but I was uncertain if some, or indeed if any of these were licensed. I very much doubted it, which is precisely why I wouldn't use them, for copyright infringements can produce very heavy fines, which I would be at great pains to avoid. There was no way that I was going down that route. I had already decided, that if I could not obtain permission to use such images, then I would use only those that I had taken myself and held my own copyright for. Even if this meant being unable to use any stills from *Kes* or anywhere else. If permission was granted however, I could screen grab them myself, but not without prior permission. I had to cover my back at all costs. Even so, I was most grateful for the information so far.

[54] The stile at the far end of Bell Ground Wood. [55] Initials carved into the trunk of a beech tree which from the date would have been present when *Kes* was filmed. [56] The Book Vault bookshop in Market Street.

Chapter 7

Sheffield University & The Barry Hines Archive
Special Collections Department
(19th January 2023)

Having now visited and photographed most of the main *Kes* original film locations, there was one more very important location that I just had to visit. This location I only discovered, again thanks to Greg Davies's *Looking for Kes* BBC documentary, which concerned The Barry Hines Archives in the Special Collections Department at Sheffield University. I didn't even know this resource existed until the documentary was shown on BBC television. However, before contacting Sheffield University, I needed to be certain that a very personalised book on *Kes*, such as the one that I was proposing, was a possibility, and I wouldn't know that until I had completed the visits to Barnsley and Hoyland Common to find and photograph enough of the original film locations. Now that this had been more or less completed, I felt more confident in approaching Sheffield University.

My first port of call was obviously Professor David Forrest, Faculty Director of Education in Film and Television Studies at Sheffield University, whom I had become aware of through Greg Davies's BBC documentary. I had already purchased his scholarly book, *Kes, Threads and Beyond*, and discovered his contact email address on the University website. I had put off this email for so long that now I began to worry. Would he respond in the affirmative? Or, if like certain others, would he respond at all? I would dearly have liked to have used a few screen shots from *Kes*, particularly as I could then demonstrate how some of the film locations have changed over time from 1968 to those that I have taken 55 years or so later. Whether Professor Forrest could help with this matter I wasn't sure.

I needn't have worried. The next day, Professor Forrest's reply came through. Not only was he very pleased to hear from me, but he also sent me the link to visiting the archives (www.sheffield.ac.uk/library/special/special).

From this site I was able to click on 'Discover Our Archives', then identify the folders that I would like to view and then I was free to contact the Special Collections Department, which is open from Monday to Thursday from 10.00am - 12.30pm and 1.30pm - 4-00pm. However, I also wanted to meet up with Professor Forrest himself to combine this with my actual visit on the day, so he advised me that before I made the appointment, to ensure that he was on campus, whereby he would sign my copy of his excellent book. I immediately opened the Special Collections website and was amazed to see the number of papers and books and artifacts held in archive. It is all housed in 10 boxes, so I made notes of the *Kes* related items to be ready when boxes, so I made notes of the *Kes* related items to be ready when Professor Forrest could get back to me with a date. As I was only writing about the film *Kes*, I didn't require access to the much more numerous items concerning Barry's other books etc., even though I would dearly have loved to have seen them. One single day wouldn't have been enough in any event.

I then received a second email from David Forrest who informed me that whilst I could take photographs of the artifacts in the archive, I almost certainly would not be able to put them in the public domain, i.e., in this book without copyright permission. Although this was disappointing, at least I could add any images taken at the archives to my personal collection of *Kes* images, which has been growing considerably for quite some time now and I would also no doubt learn more about Barry Hines himself. However, David did inform me that there is a large Billy Casper mural outside the Arts Tower, along with several of Barry Hines's quotes in the library, and I was free to use any of these as I wished. In truth, it would be a privilege just to view any of the artifacts in the archives and I would be more than happy to use just the mural and quotes for this work. David advised me that he was only on campus on Tuesdays and Thursdays now and would contact me as soon as a suitable date could be arranged for me to visit. In the meantime, I closely studied the archive's website and, despite wishing to add many of the items to my desiderata, it soon became obvious that I would have to restrict my requirements to items relating purely to *Kes* and therefore not wishing to appear greedy and wasting staff time, I made a short-list of the most desirable items that I desired to photograph, which ran as follows:

1. The Arts Tower, Sheffield University, 12 Bolsover Street, Sheffield (S3 7NA).

2. The Billy Casper mural outside the Arts Tower.

3. Barry Hines's quotes in the library.

4. Professor David Forrest outside the Arts Tower.

5. Professor David Forrest signing my copy of his book *Kes, Threads & Beyond*.

6. Professor David Forrest with me outside the Arts Tower.

7. Barry Hines's scarf, knitted for him by an aunt.

8. Barry Hines's school report, plus all of the following:

Special Collections Catalogue Hines Papers

Page 7
Novel

8/1.	Manuscript 1st draft (95).
9/2.	Typescript with m.s. annotations (137).
10/2a.	Two reviews of *A Kestrel for a Knave*.

Film
3/1.   Typescript (90).
3/2.   Folder containing call sheet, 3 still photographs etc.

Page 8
Play
3/3.   Folder of articles and correspondence etc.

Page 9
Musical
19.   Poster for *Kes*.

Addenda
24.   *Kes* related newspaper articles from Barnsley Chronicle.
25.   Manuscript notes by Barry Hines for talk on *Kes*.
27.   Summary of research project undertaken by Charlie Pritchard Brennan's Year 8 English class at Hinde's House School, 2013.

I sent this list off to the Archives just before Christmas 2022 and received an almost immediate reply plus a booking form to itemise the artefacts that I wished to peruse, using this form. I also selected Thursday 19th January 2023 for my intended visit. I filled in the booking form as requested and the date and artifacts were duly confirmed. I also let David Forrest know and we planned to meet up on the day. I couldn't wait for the day to arrive.

However, before visiting Sheffield University, there was another location that I particularly desired to place on film. This concerned the former ABC cinema in the town of Doncaster which was where *Kes* received its world premiere. I wasn't even sure that the building still survived, for it had apparently been derelict for around the past thirty years. However, as Doncaster was only an hour or so away from my home, I believed it was worth the effort to try and find the exact location at least, for it was an important part of the *Kes* story. Scrutinising the internet, I discovered to my great joy that the building was still there, albeit in a derelict state. I also discovered that it was located on Cleveland Street (DN1 3EH). Once this information had been secured, on 2nd January 2023, my wife Gill and I set off up the M1 and then the M18 motorway for Doncaster. Just over an hour later, on a cold but sunny morning, I parked the car on a side-road off Cleveland Street, grabbed my camera and walked back to Cleveland Street. There were many large buildings on Cleveland Street, so to save time, I asked a passer-by if he knew where the old cinema was located. He told me that it was only a hundred yards or so further along the street on the left-hand side. Thanking him, I made my way in the direction he so kindly pointed out to me. I already knew what I was looking for, as I had studied images of the place on the internet, but just to be one hundred percent certain that I had the right building in front of me, I had placed a photograph of it from the internet on to my mobile phone, and as I approached the site, I identified it immediately. I didn't need the internet image but still checked it to be certain. To be fair, the building appeared to be in reasonable shape and wasn't nearly as derelict as I had feared, or at least, externally. In fact, to my surprise, the ground floor section was occupied with factory shops. I wasn't expecting that. At the time of my visit, virtually all the surrounding road systems were undergoing massive roadworks, all dug up and covered with bright red coloured barriers, which rendered photography a trifle more awkward than it ought to have been. However, less than five minutes later, I had secured enough images for both my *Kes* talk and this book. So that was another location of the *Kes* story safely recorded. As I studied the building, I couldn't help but imagine the scene back in 1970 on Wednesday 25th March, when most of the cast, crew and invited guests entered this building for the world premiere of this soon to become famous film. How I would have loved to have been present on this occasion. I wondered if they had a red carpet laid out. I expect they did. I took a few more photographs of the building and we then set off back down the motorway to download the new images onto my computer.

Then came the long-awaited day when I would be meeting with Professor David Forrest at Sheffield University. Again, my son David accompanied me, and I am so pleased that he did because he took many photographs for me that I couldn't take myself, because I would be present in the resulting images. I am not a big fan of having my photograph taken I must admit, but for my book, I believe it was important to show that I had visited these locations myself and not just copied the images from the internet etc. As usual, we set off up the M1 motorway early on the 19th January on a bitterly cold and frosty morning. By the time we reached the motorway, the sun had broken through and so yet again, we had glorious sunshine with us the whole day. Unfortunately, we also had to contend with a freezing cold wind once we arrived in Sheffield. We came off the motorway at the junction for Sheffield Meadowhall, a large shopping complex where part of *The Full Monty* was filmed. We then bypassed Sheffield Wednesday football ground at Hillsborough, where almost one hundred people died when the stand collapsed many years ago. I was surprised at the number of high-rise buildings that had grown up in and around Sheffield, for it is many years since I paid the city a visit and this episode had been due to an invite from the well-known ornithologist and author, Professor Tim Birkhead, a senior lecturer, and reader in zoology at Sheffield University. Tim was giving a talk on birds, and he asked me to take along my trained male golden eagle Star. Since then, I have only bypassed Sheffield, usually on the M1 on my way to Barnsley and Hoyland Common.

Before long, the satnav heralded our arrival at the Arts Tower, and what an amazing building this is. We drove up to the barrier and pressed the speaker button to ask for the barrier to be raised, so that we could progress to the car park. It wasn't quite that simple. We were told that we needed a permit and had we got one? I replied that we had an appointment to see Professor David Forrest, but even so, we were told that we would have to ask David for a permit, otherwise, we would get a parking fine. However, the barrier was duly raised, and we found a parking space beside the front entrance to the Arts Tower, where we instantly saw David Forrest waiting for us. David strongly advised us to retrace our steps, drive back the way we had come and park in one of the nearby side streets, as he did not have a permit for us, and as we were going to be present for several hours, we would almost certainly get a parking fine. We took David's advice and soon found a suitable parking space only a stone's throw away in a side-street and then set off on foot back to the Arts Tower. We spotted a car on our way towards the Arts Tower that had just received a parking ticket, so we were very pleased that we had heeded David's advice. I only mention this to prewarn others who may wish to follow in our footsteps.

We then walked up the steps of the Arts Tower and shook hands with David, whom I was very pleased to meet, after seeing him on Greg Davies's *Looking for Kes*. After shaking hands David proceeded to inform us about Barry Hines and his connection with the Arts Tower. It was from his office on the 9th floor of the tower that he wrote another of his novels, entitled *The Gamekeeper*. Although Barry heralded from a working-class background, it appeared that he enjoyed working within the walls of academia. It was then that David told us about the *Looking for Kes* film shoot. Since viewing the latter several times, I was always of the opinion that the Barry Hines Archive was housed in the Arts Tower, for that is the impression that the documentary implies, and anyone could be forgiven for arriving at this conclusion. However, this is not so, for it is housed in the Western Bank Library that runs alongside the Arts Tower on the opposite side of the road [57]. This was a revelation that I was certainly not expecting. Although the footage of this part of *Looking for Kes* was indeed filmed in the Arts Tower, it apparently transpired that the lighting in the library was not conducive to filming the scenes that the BBC required, so, three items were temporarily transferred from the library to the tower. Of the three items that were transferred, one was the first, handwritten draft of *A Kestrel for a Knave*, plus Barry Hines's scarf that was knitted for him by an aunt, and finally, Barry's final school report. When I first contacted the archives, they could not locate the school report and I was so overawed with everything taking place, I forgot to ask David where it might now be located. David proceeded to give us many details of Barry's time at the Arts Tower and by the time he had finished, we were all freezing to death from the harsh cold wind that blew between the two buildings, which acted just like a wind tunnel. I needed a few shots of David and myself outside the Arts Tower and this was accomplished by my son David. After a while, David Forrest took us over to the library foyer for our much-awaited visit. Before visiting the archives however, David very kindly signed my copy of his book, and I signed a copy of my 'eagle falconry' book for him [58]. David told us that he was working on a new Barry Hines book which I cannot wait to see. Unfortunately, David had work to attend to, so after leaving our midst, he gave us directions to follow for the archives. What a lovely man. It was fantastic to meet a person who is, if anything, even more keen on the *Kes* story than I am, and believe me, that is saying something.

After David left us, we then climbed the stairs to speak to a receptionist behind a desk. Once we told her of our mission, she let us through a type of turnstile barrier and from there, we entered a room where a lovely young lady named Eleanor Mulkeen-Parker was awaiting our arrival [59]. We also met Laura Smith Brown, Special Collections Manager, who had so very kindly arranged the items for me to photograph. On two tables, placed side by side, Eleanor showed us four large cardboard boxes. One of these was grey in colour and was twice the size of the other three buff-coloured boxes. These boxes contained all the items that I had asked for, and I couldn't wait to begin looking through them.

In the first of the three smaller cardboard boxes I discovered the one item that I desired to view most of all. This was the first handwritten draft of *A Kestrel for a Knave* [60]. I had seen images of the first page of this draft on the internet and I well remember Greg Davies handling this very sheet. The manuscript was housed in a pale-yellow folder, from which I very carefully extracted this treasure. This was like finding the Holy Grail for a religious person. I simply couldn't believe that I was now handling this in person. My hands were almost trembling with wonderment. It is a very long time since I have experienced a buzz like that. Never, in my wildest dreams did I think that I would ever see this artifact, let alone be allowed to handle it. If I saw nothing else that day, this manuscript made the Sheffield trip doubly worthwhile. I placed the manuscript on the table and lifted the first page. Having seen images of it several times, it was like handling an old friend. Many may believe that this aspect of my response to handling this treasure to be rather excessive, but anyone who fully understands the sheer, deep interest I have in such things, will realise the reason for my rather emotional behaviour. I photographed a couple of dozen pages and would have preferred to photograph the whole manuscript, but I also needed to photograph all the other artifacts as well. Even though I had booked the artifacts for the whole day, I needed to go to Hoyland Common as I had a yearning to photograph the far side of Bell Ground Wood where Billy Casper climbed a five barred gate in his search for Kes. I should have done this on my previous visit but didn't think of it until much later, so, I wished to correct this hindsight whilst I was within striking range.

But I digress. As I examined the manuscript, I became aware of the fact that Barry Hines had crossed out many sections and used at least three different coloured inks, namely blue, black and red. I read many passages as I sorted through the pages and not only the book, but the film images resonated from these pages before me. As I read the lines, flashbacks of *Kes* emerged in my mind. It was an amazing experience. The lighting in the room was acceptable for me, but of course, the inverse square law was invoked. Any photographer worthy of the name knows this law. It is when the light falling onto a surface from a single light source gradually decreases when one part of the length of a page for example, as in this case, is furthest from the light source. This causes problems for cameras, because the light is uneven across the whole page and thus, it would have been preferable to have taken a scanner with me, as the light from a scanner, as its name implies, evenly scans the page with the same light intensity over the entire surface. I didn't have a scanner with me, so had to work as best as I could. As well as crossing sections out, Barry had also added smaller pieces of paper with parts of the story added to a page and held in place with paper clips. This was often how books were written before the use of computers. Today, we can simply add new text wherever needed by the cut and paste technique, or simply adding to the text at any point by placing the cursor in the required place, which is an absolute boon to modern authors. For me personally though, there is nothing like handling original handwritten documents from the past. Few authors today, if any, now handwrite manuscripts. We seldom even handwrite letters these days because of computer email technology and so these items are rapidly becoming a thing of the past. It is mostly electronic mail today and unless we print off hard copies on paper, all the latter are effectively in cyberspace and are almost never signed in the author's own hand. This lacks the personal touch for me, and so viewing this priceless artifact was something very, very special and something I will never forget.

I was so engrossed that I spent the best part of an hour photographing this wonderful artifact and then suddenly remembered that I needed to view and photograph all the other items in the four boxes. I didn't realise until later that my son David was also photographing me photographing the items as I lifted them from the boxes, for which I was very grateful, but at this point I was not to know how grateful, for it later transpired that I would be unable to use the images of the documents for this publication due to the Agency and the Barry Hines Trust which did not reply to my request for such. Fortunately, I could use the one's that David took of me simply holding the documents. I would have loved to have had the opportunity to use many of the photographs that I took in the archives, especially after taking the trouble to visit the collection.

I then opened the large grey box which contained, amongst other artifacts, Barry Hines's scarf that his aunt had knitted for him **[61]**. Like the manuscript, I had seen images of this on the internet and remember Greg Davies not only handling this scarf but sniffing it as well. He said it reminded him of the aroma of his own school days. This was yet another artifact that I was so desperate to see, handle and photograph, and I was not to be disappointed. I was enjoying every single minute of this day. Also in the grey box was a large and a smaller *Kes* poster, a few playhouse posters where *Kes* had been performed as a stage play, one being entitled *Kes Is Coming Home*, written by Barry Hines and adapted for the stage by Lawrence Till for The Academy Theatre, Birdwell, Barnsley, for the 40th anniversary of *Kes*. Another was a poster for the Nottingham Playhouse where a stage production had taken place. Also, in the box there was a black baseball type cap that had been given to Barry Hines by the crew of *Kes* back in 1968. The cap bore the legend in gold lettering, 'Born Kicking' and showed signs of wear. I never previously knew of the existence of this cap, or indeed, many of the artifacts that I was to discover within the boxes.

I then returned to the first box, where I photographed a few sections of a typed manuscript for *A Kestrel for a Knave*. This manuscript also contained a few handwritten annotations, probably in Barry's own hand. At this point, Eleanor showed great interest in our quest, and she came and joined us. I had my laptop with us and showed her sections of my 'Discovering *Kes*' lecture. Eleanor hadn't seen the film but planned to obtain a copy on DVD. We had a great conversation, and she was a wonderful help to us. David photographed the two of us beside the boxes of artifacts.

Several *Kes* related press cuttings were next to face the camera, most of which I had never seen before. One was from *The Observer* and others were from *The Guardian* and some more from local newspapers. The next item was especially interesting. This was Barry Hines's own personal original draft screenplay for *Kes*. It was encased in a burgundy-coloured folder, identical to one that I had recently seen up for sale during my research. The one for sale was 91 pages in length and was offered by Royal Books Inc. in the USA. It sold for £3,992.85. Just imagine how much Barry Hines's own personal copy would sell for if it ever came on the market. Of course, that is highly unlikely to happen, and I am so pleased that it won't, because all these items are kept in the safe custody at Sheffield. I am a great believer in such items being held by museums and special collections departments, rather than by private collectors, because once in the hands of the latter, nobody else can get to see and examine them, therefore, serious research is often completely hampered because of their unavailability.

Next to emerge from the box was a *Kes* call sheet No. 42, printed on light blue paper. This sheet is dated Wednesday, 21st August 1968 and concerned some of the actor's arrivals at the Queens Hotel, which was situated on Regent Street in Barnsley (S70 2HP). This hotel is now permanently closed but was immediately earmarked for another shoot list that I needed to complete in the not-too-distant future. Other locations in this document included: 56 Parkside Road and the field behind 124 Hoyland Road for Mr. Farthing's visit to watch Billy fly Kes and a possibility of a shoot at St. Helen's County Secondary School where 20 schoolchildren would be required. David 'Dai' Bradley was to be collected at 7.45am and taken to the Queens Hotel.

A footnote on the document reads:

> Canteen: H.A.P. Catering for unit, Morning break, lunch, afternoon break for 35 - 40 persons (or 55 – 60 persons).
>
> Transport: CAMERA CAR/SOUND CAR/GENERATOR/STANDBY LORRY/UNIT CARS.

This document was a fascinating insight into the world of film making and I was delighted to be given the privilege of viewing this iconic piece of *Kes* memorabilia.

Several more press cuttings and other documents involving *Kes* were found in the boxes, but to mention them all here would perhaps be too repetitive. So here are a few. There was a copy of *The Barnsley Chronicle* 2009 autumn edition which carried an article entitled *Life After Kes*, by Pamela Watford and which featured the ongoing career of

David 'Dai' Bradley. Then I discovered another call sheet. This was listed as call sheet No. 1, when the film was still entitled *A Kestrel for a Knave*, and dated 28th June 1968. This time the location was at Monastery Farm, Old Hall Farm, Hoyland Nether, with a Unit Call for 2.00pm on location. David Bradley was due on set at 4.45pm. Action props consisted of 3 baby kestrels and falconer. Special requirements: Cherry picker, ladder from Barnsley Fire Brigade and two mountaineers with safety equipment. Canteen: Local cafeteria. Transport: Camera car and unit cars.

This call sheet was of special interest to me, because for a long time, I had wondered about the scene where Billy Casper takes his kestrel from the ruins of Tankersley Old Hall, and always believed that it was probably one of the very first scenes that the film crew had shot as a priority and the date of 28th June highlighted this. I had long held this belief for two very good reasons. First, if the crew had delayed the shoot, by even two or three weeks, the young kestrel's down feathers, indicating that it was a nestling, would have been shed and the bird would have become hard-penned, or nearly so. That is to say that its primary and tail feathers would have developed sufficiently for it to fly, rendering any attempt to film Billy taking his kestrel would have been null and void. The instant that Richard Hines placed the bird back into its nesting hole, it would have immediately taken wing, exited the hole and flown away across the neighbouring fields and woods, never to be seen again. Richard Hines, of course, knew this, and I am sure he would have pressed the point on Ken Loach and Tony Garnett. Had the opportunity been missed, the film could not have been completed that summer of 1968 and the scene would have to be shot the following year, which would have been out of the question. The second reason was that the bird would have been fully developed and unconvincing as a newly taken chick, or eyas. This is one of the parts of film making that I find interesting, whereby scenes are often not shot in the same sequence as the original book or script. Sometimes, the end is shot before the beginning. Finding this call sheet confirmed my original thoughts and I was so pleased to have seen it.

There were several letters to Barry Hines, some from the BBC offering to dramatize *Kes* in some way. There were also three or four printed scripts for stage shows, using adaptations from the original story. There were also *Kes* musical adaptations. One of which was performed at the Bolton Octagon Theatre for The Festival of Arts and Culture which ran from Thursday 14th September until Saturday 14th October 1995. There was also a letter from Warsaw, Poland, informing Peter Crouch Plays Ltd. about a Polish edition of *A Kestrel for a Knave* that had been produced to the tune of 19,740 copies. I also found an envelope bearing an address which was just around the corner from where I live in Nottingham. The letter was addressed to Barry Hines at 96 Rugby Road, West Bridgford, Nottinghamshire. This grabbed my attention immediately. I never knew Barry had lived at this address, or even in Nottingham, even if only for a short time. The postmark stated that the letter had been posted on 7.1.1975. I was intrigued, what was Barry doing in Nottingham at that date? I knew that a stage production of *Kes* had been performed at Nottingham Playhouse and another at Nottingham Theatre Royal, and Barry had been in attendance for at least the one staged at the Playhouse, so I presumed that perhaps he was residing here for the duration of the play [62].

I knew about this play because of a good falconer friend of mine, Chris Miller, had used his kestrel as part of the performance and who had taken part in the production at Nottingham Playhouse in May 1984. Chris had told me about this during my research for this book. He had even met Barry Hines, who was in attendance for the play, which was something that I had failed to do. In the archives, there was a poster featuring just such an event. Upon my return to Nottingham, I investigated this address in West Bridgford a little further. I hadn't had time to photograph the Nottingham Playhouse poster in the archives, so I emailed Eleanor to ask if she could check the dates for me to enquire if the dates on the poster corresponded to the date on the letter, which was 1975. Eleanor very quickly answered my call and informed me that the poster dates were 17th May until 9th of June with a preview on the 16th of May, but there was no year date on the poster. The archive records gave 1984 as the probable year, which was a date mismatch for the envelope postmark, so more research was required as to why Barry was at West Bridgford, Nottinghamshire in 1975. However, I spoke to Chris Miller again and he confirmed that the production that he attended was either in 1984 or 1985, he wasn't sure of the exact year. He also informed me that the pantomime actor and writer, Kenneth Alan Taylor, who worked for 36 years at the Nottingham Playhouse was also present at this performance. Further during rehearsals, he flew the kestrel on stage to the young actor playing Billy Casper, and all went well. But when the production began for real, the powers that be pulled the flying sequences because they were concerned that the bird might land on someone's head in the audience, so instead, they simply allowed the actor to hold the kestrel and then walk off the stage to hand the bird to Chris, who was standing out of sight in the wings, rather than allow it to fly to Chris and vice-versa. This was no doubt due to health and safety reasons. I believe it was Kenneth Alan Taylor who first brought the stage version of *Kes* to the Nottingham Playhouse in May 1984. Chris very kindly sent me a photograph, possibly taken by a *Nottingham Evening Post* photographer, or a freelance photographer, which features a kestrel just about to alight on Chris's glove on the left of the frame, whilst on the right is Kenneth Alan Taylor himself [63]. The third person in the centre is the young actor who played the part of Billy Casper in the play. This image was taken in the churchyard at Radford in Nottingham. So, this information demonstrated to me that the address that I had for Barry Hines in West Bridgford, Nottingham, had nothing to do with his appearance at Nottingham Playhouse at that time. Which of course, still left me with a problem. Why was Barry Hines residing at 96 Rugby Road, West Bridgford in 1975 in the first place? I still hadn't worked out this one yet, but the answer was soon forthcoming.

I thought long and hard about where to go next with this query and then remembered that Professor David Forrest of Sheffield University had informed me that he was writing a new book about Barry Hines. If anybody knew the answer to my question, I was sure that David would be a good candidate, after all, had he not written *Barry Hines, Kes,*

Threads and Beyond? So, I emailed David with my request and yet again, he came up trumps and was most certainly able to answer my query. It transpired that Barry Hines was living at 96 Rugby Road, West Bridgford in Nottingham with his partner at the time, Jean Penchion, who was a schoolteacher in Nottingham. This was a huge surprise to me. I knew nothing about this. I had been working along the wrong lines and I had no idea that Barry and his first wife, Margaret, had parted so soon after the production of *Kes* and I had never heard of Jean Penchion before. Ronnie Steele of the Kes Group then informed me that he had met Jean Penchion at Barry Hines's funeral and he told me that she was a lovely lady. This story was taking me down more unexpected roads than I could have possibly imagined. David had also informed me that Barry and Jean later moved to Sheffield, living in the suburb of Broomhall, which is quite close to Sheffield University. I already had an address for Barry in Sheffield through a letter I had photographed in the Special Collections Department and after I gave a talk on 3rd April 2023 on British Wildflowers to Florilegium Brittanicum (a very interesting botanical artists group) at Sheffield Botanic Gardens, I decided that as I was in the area, I would pay a visit to Barry's former Sheffield address at 323 Fulwood Road (S10 3BJ). Barry had certainly moved about a bit during his lifetime. However, once I arrived on Fulwood Road, I discovered yet another anomaly. Something weird had occurred. I parked up on a side road and made my way along Fulwood Road until I came to number 325. So far so good. I expected that the next house along would be 323, Barry's former home. There it all went pear-shaped, for there was no number 323. The next house was number 321a then number 321. What was going on here, I wondered? There was a narrow alleyway at the side of these two houses, so I ventured along this until I came out at the rear of number 321a, which is where 323 ought to have been. Scaffolding had been erected all around the building **[64]**. The houses were of some vintage, so a new build wasn't the answer. I pondered for some time and decided to photograph 321a anyway because for some reason, the number had obviously been changed, and recently too judging by the new number plate on the back door, but as to why, I had no idea. 321a surely must have been the same house that was formerly Barry Hines's home. I even tried number 232, just in case I had somehow got the wrong number combination. This was now a Morrison's supermarket which was situated further down on the opposite side of the road. However, when I checked the letter upon my return home, the Sheffield University archives showed 323 as the correct address for Barry Hines and it was dated 1988, so the Morrison's supermarket building was not the one I was searching for. David Forrest had informed me that Barry had moved from Nottingham to Broomhall and this must have been at some stage after leaving his residence in West Bridgford but I have no idea yet as to what year this could be.

The West Bridgford address then threw up another anomaly. According to the blue plaque affixed to the wall of one of Barry Hine's former homes at Hoyland Common, Barry was living at this latter address from 1970 to 1976. My quandary was that according to the letter and an envelope, postmarked 07.01.1975, Barry was now living at

West Bridgford in January 1975, not on Hoyland Road as the blue plaque indicated [65]. These dates did not tally at all. It was becoming quite a detective story and I couldn't ask Barry about it as he had sadly passed away, so the next best person to ask would again be Professor David Forrest of Sheffield University. I sent David an email with my request, but in the meantime, I drove the couple of miles or so from my home to find Rugby Road and photograph number 96. Unbeknown to me, I had passed this house numerous times in the past, for it is on the same road as the recycling centre that I often use. The house was an unassuming, typical small-town dwelling, with an equally small front garden and a garage affixed to the front. How long Barry Hines had lived at this address, again, I have currently no idea. One thing was for sure, my quest was throwing up more questions than answers. Later, although I am not sure exactly when, they moved to Broomhall which is quite close to the university, where Barry was now working. David Forrest, in answer to my query about the house in Broomhall, wondered if 323 Fulwood Road had been converted to flats, which was a distinct possibility that I hadn't considered. As aforementioned, it was certainly surrounded with scaffolding during my visit, indicating that much work was in progress and maybe flat conversion was part of this?

In the archives was also a poster featuring a dance-theatre adaptation by Jonathon Watkins which was performed at the Sheffield Crucible and the archives hold Eleanor Mulvey's personal admission ticket. Eleanor, of course, was Barry's second wife. I photographed virtually all the items in the boxes, but my camera batteries were beginning to run low, and I still desired to photograph other aspects for this book over in Hoyland Common whilst I was in the area. I would have loved to have photographed every page of every document, but such would require another visit plus spare batteries to complete this mission.

From the beginning, I particularly desired to photograph the Arts Tower and its attendant Billy Casper mural. We had already seen this when we first met up with David Forrest, but the sunlight on the windows was too harsh then, with bright sunlight reflecting from the windows directly into the camera lens causing flare. Now though, the sun had moved across the sky, and we were able to get images of the mural and some quotes by Barry Hines that are adhered to the windows of the Arts Tower [66]. Both David and I fancied a session in the Paternoster lift, which is one of only a few surviving examples in the country. I had seen Greg Davies use this lift with David Forrest in *Looking for Kes*. One must jump quickly on this contraption as it is constantly in motion. Not ideal for disabled people I have to say. Unfortunately, the lift was out of action with a red warning strap positioned across the entrance. I must admit, I felt a bit disappointed, for I would have loved to have travelled to the top of this amazing building. All of Sheffield and far beyond must be visible from that stunning height. Oh well, another time perhaps.

So now it was time to take our leave of Sheffield, but what an experience we had shared. I will never forget it. Whilst at the archives, I had noticed another address at

Hoyland Common where Barry Hines had apparently lived. This was 32 Hoyland Road, so I thought it worthwhile to record this in the camera along with everything else we had photographed. But that was only one reason why I desired to return to Hoyland Common. The main reason was to photograph the area at Bell Ground Wood where Billy Casper had searched for Kes, before discovering that Jud had 'killed' the bird.

In this scene, Billy enters the garden, only to discover that the mews door is swinging ajar and stepping inside, he realises that Kes is missing. His first thoughts are that Kes has escaped, so he grabs the lure and wanders along the roads and streets around his home and then across the fields, searching for her, swinging the lure, and calling for her constantly as he goes.

"Come on Kes, come on girl," he repeatedly shouts, but there is no response.

He even wanders as far as Bell Ground Wood, climbing atop a five-barred gate to obtain some elevation whilst swinging the lure, but there is still no sign of Kes. Jumping off the top of the gate, Billy wanders through Bell Ground Wood and out the other side to Tankersley Old Hall, from where he originally obtained Kes. There was no sign of her anywhere. Billy is distraught and becoming frantic with worry. Where is she? Still swinging the lure, he searches high and low, hoping she will see the lure and return. But nothing was stirring. He wanders back through Bell Ground Wood towards home when an awful reality suddenly dawns on him. Jud! He's done something to her. With this sickening thought in his mind, Billy heads rapidly for home, ready to confront Jud head-on, his former fear of him now abated somewhat.

Back at home, he bursts in and sees Jud sitting at the kitchen table, calmly having some lunch. Immediately, Billy accuses Jud of doing something with Kes.

"You've killed her," Billy screams, "I know you 'ave."

"So, what if I 'ave, it was bitin" and scratchin" me, I had to kill it," yells Jud.

Mrs. Casper interjects, "You never 'ave, you 'aven't killed that poor lad's bird?"

Billy is beside himself and launches a full-scale attack on Jud. Jud of course, being bigger and more powerful, soon overcomes Billy's weedy frame. Mrs. Casper pulls Billy away and shouts at Jud, "What 'ave you killed his bird for, 'as he done summat?"

Jud scowls, "As he done summat? I'll say he 'as, if he 'ad put the bets on like I told him to, this would never 'ave 'appened."

Mrs. Casper, slightly taken aback says, "Why, did they win or summat?"

Jud responds, "Did they win? I would 'ave won a tenner at least. I could 'ave had a week off work wi' that."

Billy screams and throws himself on the sofa.

"There were no need to tek it out on Kes, you could a teken it out on me," rants Billy.

Mrs. Casper asks Jud what he has done with the bird.

"I threw it in bin," he yells.

Billy gets up from the sofa and rushes out to two dustbins near the back door. There is nothing in the first, but when he lifts the lid off the second bin, Billy slowly places both hands inside and gently lifts Kes's lifeless body from the bin. He smoothes over Kes's ruffled feathers and heartbreakingly carefully folds her limp wings alongside her body. His face now contorted with rage, Billy rushes back inside, and swinging Kes around by her jesses, he tries to hit Jud with her lifeless corpse. Mrs. Casper, by this time has had enough of the pair of them and orders Billy to take the bird outside, which he eventually does. Billy finds an axe in the shed and then finds a suitable spot beneath a hedge, digs a small grave and sadly lays Kes to rest.

This scene concludes the film, which some have criticised for its sad ending, (most people prefer a happy ending I guess) and we are left wondering what would happen to Billy now? *A Kestrel for a Knave* has a different ending, but the producer and director decided to leave that out of the screenplay, because it would have required too many flashbacks that would perhaps have been difficult to film and edit. I think they made the right choice. David 'Dai' Bradley played his part of Kes's demise wonderfully, but he was informed beforehand that they would have to kill one of the three kestrels they had been using for the closing scenes. David had spent weeks with these birds and was horrified that they had killed one of them, just for a film. This was Ken Loach's plan to obtain realism from the actor, just like in the caning sequence. They didn't of course, kill any of the kestrels, that was never going to happen, but Ken was not going to tell that to David, because he wanted a natural reaction, which he may not have got had David known the secret beforehand. The latter apparently only found out the truth once all the required footage was in the can. Freddie Fletcher, who played the part of Jud, has said with some conviction that David had no idea at first that the dead kestrel wasn't one of the three used in the film. Ken Loach had approached Richard Hines and Freddie Fletcher and told them within earshot of David 'Dai' Bradley, whilst in the queue for the canteen, to go and 'kill' one of the kestrels ready for the next scene.

So, where did the dead kestrel come from? I only recently discovered the truth behind this after I had purchased a first edition copy of *Life After Kes*. This is a very useful book for any *Kes* scholars, and it certainly highlighted many points for me, particularly this one. The reality is that the dead kestrel was supplied by my good friend of over half a century, John Bishop Murray, who at the time worked as a taxidermist at the Royal Scottish Museum in Edinburgh [67 & 68]. So, my knowing John Murray personally was a second personal link I had to this amazing film. Once I discovered this fact, I spoke to John about it, and he confirmed that it was true. I had known John all these years and yet I never had an inkling that he had been involved with *Kes*. Ken Loach, or one of his crew, contacted the good offices of the British Falconers Club (BFC) of which I have been a member since 2006, in an attempt to find a source for a dead kestrel and it transpired that

John, a BFC member and falconry consultant for the Scottish Home Office, as well as a gifted taxidermist, and anthropologist, happened to have one in his freezer, so he sent the bird, packed in ice to the film crew in Barnsley. Ken did a great job of convincing David 'Dai' Bradley that the dead bird was none other than Hardy (he apparently didn't notice the difference), and it worked for David gave a very realistic performance, even though it seemed a cruel way to achieve this end. This is often how Ken Loach worked, sometimes only giving out partial scripts to the actors to allow for some natural ad-libbing for realistic effect. Much of the scene where Billy meets the farmer at Tankersley Old Hall is ad-libbed to a large extent, as also was the library scene and this allows for much more realism from the actors. Thus ended, in my humble opinion, one of the finest films ever made.

But one question still niggled me. Nobody, so far as I am aware, has asked what subsequently happened to the corpse of the kestrel used for the end of the film.? Possibly because nobody had been bothered enough or, more likely, never had even thought about it, but my enquiring mind was now running on overdrive. I wanted to know for sure. Was it really buried beneath the hedge as we are shown in the film, was it simply discarded, ending up being left in the dustbin, or was it sent back to John Murray in Edinburgh? I was hoping that it had been mounted by a taxidermist, perhaps by John Murray himself, because it is a splendid piece of cinematic history that I have ever since believed should have been preserved for posterity. The only person known to me personally that could answer this question, was of course John Murray himself, so I lost no time in asking John what indeed had become of the deceased kestrel? Did he get it back again? John's reply was not exactly what I was expecting or hoping for. It transpired that the dead kestrel sadly remained in the dustbin as it was a bit of a mess when John gave it to them, so he did not want it back, even though it was one of his own kestrels, a little female that just keeled over one night after her flying exercise. John could not get her to a suitable avian vet in Glasgow quickly enough and sadly she quickly passed away, so he simply placed her in the museum freezer, presumably to mount her at some future date. This was a disappointment to me, and no doubt for John too, but then, nobody, but nobody back in 1968 had the faintest idea as to how popular *A Kestrel for a Knave* and ultimately the film *Kes* was going to become. What a pity though, for John, or an equally skilled taxidermist could no doubt have tidied up her body, imped (replaced) any damaged primary or tail feathers and preserved her for posterity. I really had hoped that John had asked for the deceased kestrel to be returned to him after filming ceased, at least, it would probably still exist as a mounted specimen. That would have been nice. However, one must be realistic here. Nobody apparently ever gave a minute's thought as to whether the dead kestrel could so easily have become a much loved and important cinematic icon which hopefully could eventually have found its way into a local museum or perhaps even The Barry Hines Archives and kept for future generations to admire. What a shame and what a lost opportunity to have such an important piece of cinematic history merely left to rot in a dustbin and ultimately find its way to a local landfill site. So, the last kestrel to appear in *Kes*, did so posthumously.

While I was ruminating over the demise of John Murray's kestrel and because John had played a significant part in the *Kes* finale, I was desirous of including an image of John within the pages of this work. Over the years, John has sent me many images of himself with various eagles, hawks, and owls on his glove, but I noted that I couldn't remember any images of him with a kestrel, so I asked him if any photographs of him with a kestrel still survived. John searched through his archives and sent me an image of him holding a kestrel in full colour. This was a very nice image, but the kestrel didn't look right, not to me anyway. I deduced it could only be one of three options. It was either a melanic, or dark form of the Eurasian kestrel *(Falco tinnunculus)*, an African Grey kestrel *(Falco ardosiaceus)*, my preferred option, or a Dickinson's kestrel *(Falco dickinsoni)*. In the next email, John confirmed that the bird was indeed an African Grey kestrel, but it at least was a kestrel, but then I noticed another email attachment that John had sent. I opened this and to my very pleasant surprise, it was a photograph of an old newspaper article of John with a Eurasian kestrel. And it got even better. The kestrel in the image was not only a Eurasian kestrel, but it was also the brother of the dead one that John had sent to the film crew. This was amazing. Because the photograph was in the form of a newspaper illustration, it was not as sharp as I would have liked, but then again, we are going back to the 1960s and it was printed on newspaper, so some graininess was to be expected. It was yet another twist in the tale of this wonderful saga. This photograph just had to be included in *Discovering Kes*. Although it wasn't the actual bird used in *Kes*, it was most certainly the next best thing. John told me that he thought his father had taken the original photograph. As a matter of interest, John informed me that the African Grey kestrel had arrived in a Glasgow fruit market, rather remarkably with a bunch of bananas and was sent to John, who was then living in digs, and which dates the picture to 1964. How the kestrel survived the journey and arrived in Britain still alive is nothing short of remarkable. John trained it and took three starlings with it. Then, the person who gave it to John wanted it back again, so John had to relinquish the bird. The owner soon became fed up with it and it eventually ended up in Edinburgh Zoo. Later, searching through my image library, I discovered a photograph of John Murray with a kestrel that he had sent me many years previously and which I had forgotten all about. Was this the kestrel from the film or one of its siblings? It turned out it was neither, for this kestrel was a much earlier specimen from the early 1960s. Even so, it was a good image of John and one that I decided I might select for this volume.

But I digress. After leaving Sheffield University and the archives, I needed to discover if Caspers Fish & Chips shop had new tenants, or not. So, after lunch at a McDonalds on the Birdwell to Hoyland Common Road, we set our sights for the chip shop. To my dismay, nothing had changed since our last visit, except this time, we parked the car and peered through the windows. All the framed and signed *Kes* and Billy Casper photographs had been removed. Dave Rose did inform me that whoever bought the business, would have the opportunity to purchase the *Kes* photograph collection for £1000, or he would take them away with him. It seemed like the latter scenario had occurred. Although I half expected this, I must confess my disappointment, for it seemed to seal the fate of Caspers once and for all. Alas, the end of an era was in plain sight. I am only grateful for the times we visited the shop in happier days. All the Casper signage was still in place on the exterior of the shop walls, but I do fear for its future. I sincerely hope that someone has the good grace to save the shop signs and put them in a museum, or something similar. It didn't look good. However, we did get to see it before it finally closed its doors, which was little short of a miracle really, for had I left this project any longer, we would never have had the privilege of having meals within the premises and I will be eternally grateful for that.

Rather dismally, we returned to the car and set off down Fitzwilliam Street, planning to head for the filming location at Bell Ground Wood. However, as we drove down Fitzwilliam Street, we noticed an elderly gentleman crossing the street and entering the Hoyland Common Working Men's Club. On all our previous visits, the club had been closed, which had always niggled me somewhat. Here was a chance that I was not going to let pass us by. It was open! I parked the car on the street, opposite the club doorway, grabbed my camera, and we entered the premises. It was exactly as it had appeared in Greg Davies's *Looking for Kes*. Nothing had changed, which pleased me enormously **[69]**. We spoke to a couple of staff members and explained why we were there and asked permission to take some photographs. Our request was readily granted and so I took pictures of the bar, games area and other parts of the interior. I needed to visit the toilets and as I did so, I noticed that the back door was ajar, so I peeked outside. Here, attached to the rear wall, I noticed a large poster which featured a photograph of Billy Casper sat on the crossbar of the goalpost, an image taken during the famous football sequence **[70]**. I was delighted with this. *Kes* was still remembered in Hoyland Common after all. But even better was to come. Whilst I was out the back, David had been talking to a staff member who, when I returned, led us into a function room to the side of and to the rear of the bar. At the far end of the function room was a stage and backing this was a huge England flag. The top left-hand quarter of the flag contained the Union flag, whilst the top right-hand quarter contained an image of Billy Casper with Kes on his glove **[71]**. I was delighted with this and took yet more photographs. Emerging back into the bar we met two gentlemen who had known Barry Hines personally. Both readily consented to having their photograph taken with me at the bar. We then got into a discussion with a group sat around a table and I asked them what was happening to Caspers Fish & Chips shop, but unfortunately, none of them were sure. I then mentioned my next quest concerning the Sheffield Road end of Bell Ground Wood. Here they were much more knowledgeable. We apparently needed to turn onto the Sheffield Road, heading southwards and to look out for a farm shop. Alongside this shop, we would find the footpath to the wood.

We followed the given instructions and soon came to Parkside Farm shop (S74 0EA), where we turned in to the car park. Just to be sure we were in the right place, we went into the farm shop itself, which was excellent, full of locally sourced farm produce and spoke to the owner, Bryan Mason, who proved very helpful. I showed him a screengrab on my mobile phone of Billy Casper standing on the five-barred gate looking for Kes. Bryan also owned the farm which backed onto Bell Ground Wood at this very point, and he confirmed that the scene was indeed the one I was looking for. So, my hunch was correct. I also asked Bryan about Caspers Fish & Chips shop and his reply was not encouraging. It transpired that because of all the recent increases in fuel prices, food, and very high bank interest rates, nobody was prepared to take on the business. What a shame. We had quite a long chat with Bryan and his staff who were very interested in what we were doing, and they then gave us directions to follow. We were warned that the footpath was very muddy, but there had been a hoar frost the previous night and temperatures were still not much above freezing, so we hoped the ground would not be too muddy. This was a concern as although I had brought my walking boots in the hope that we would have time to visit this location, David hadn't and I forgot to mention it to him until we were at the archives, and he was wearing new white trainers. He was not amused.

"YOU said we were working indoors at the archives. YOU said we wouldn't be working in the field this day, YOU said."

I could only apologise to him and hoped for the best. We left the car in the farm shop car park and walked back up Sheffield Road for about one hundred yards, when we came to the footpath [72]. Bryan Mason was right; it was very muddy and much of the frost had now thawed. We climbed over the stile and ventured along the narrow track, which was pock-marked with countless human footprints. I also noticed that the sun was in the wrong direction again for photography, shining as it was, directly into our eyes and camera lenses causing some flare. We were there now so we had no choice other than to make the best of it. The track became muddier as we progressed, and the scene had changed somewhat due to the building of the enormous EVRi warehouse. A huge sloping bankside had been constructed, and indeed, was still in the process of being constructed on our visit. Heavy machinery was in action, adding finishing touches to the bank. The famous five-barred gate had been located on the EVRi side of the footpath and, of course, with the construction of the steep bank and with the warehouse perched on the top, the gate had now disappeared, which I expected anyway. Half a century is a long time in the life of a five-barred gate. However, the rest of the scene was much as it had been when Ken Loach and his film crew were here in 1968. Our footwear soon became plastered with mud, but the scene was an important one for me, so we took images all along its length right up to Bell Ground Wood itself, where, due to the shade from the trees, the hoar frost remained largely still frozen. I was so pleased to have found this location, but it was now time to return to Hoyland Common to find and photograph another of Barry Hines's former residences. This was 32 Hoyland Road, which I had discovered in one of archive documents. We parked right outside Caspers Fish & Chips shop (I do love this place) and noticed some strange reflections on the shop wall. These were caused by the sun striking the house windows on the opposite side of Princess Street, but they looked most strange. One reflection closely resembled an African Maasai shield. From Caspers, we walked onto Hoyland Road and then turned left, noticing that the even numbers were on the opposite side of the road. Finally, after a short walk, we found No. 32, next door to the village community centre which occupies not only Hoyland Road but also a corner of Tinker Lane, opposite the Star public house. No. 32 Hoyland Road is an end terraced house built from stone and with a blue-grey painted front door. It seemed that Barry had lived in several different houses during his 76 years of life, at least three of them on this one side of Hoyland Road, and this was just one of them, or as far as I am aware, for I have no dates as to when he lived here, if indeed at all. We walked back along Hoyland Road and came to an alley which led to a field to the rear of this block of terraced houses. We ventured down this alley and ventured into the field. Was this one of the fields used during the filming of *Kes*? It looked familiar that's for sure. I photographed it anyway.

This had been a wonderful day. I had learned a lot and added greatly to my *Kes* image collection, which now numbered hundreds of photographs. Each trip to the area around Barnsley has become a sort of pilgrimage for me. With 32 Hoyland Road now recorded digitally, it was time to head for home and to sort through the images that we had taken. All that remained now was to contact the agency that held the copyright to the Barry Hines Archive to seek permission for me to use some of the images for this work. This was to prove more difficult than I imagined. Eleanor at the Sheffield archives emailed me with the details of the agency that apparently held the copyright for all the Barry Hines documents. So, I lost no time in trying to contact them. Unfortunately, despite accessing the agency website, I kept receiving the invalid email icon appearing on my laptop. I contacted Eleanor again at the archives and explained my problem and bless her, she did some research and sent me the contact details of three people who worked at the agency. Almost immediately, Jessica Hare at the agency contacted me to ask me for some more information. First, was I planning to self-publish, or approach a publisher and second, could I provide a full inventory of the photographed items? If I provided the answers to the above, then the agency would discuss the matter with the Barry Hines Estate. This seemed fair enough, so I replied that I was planning to use an established publisher and sent a list of the items that I wished to use for this book. I also sent three of the photographs taken by my son David of myself holding Barry Hines's scarf, the folder housing the original manuscript and Barry Hines's copy of the script for *Kes*. It was then simply a matter of waiting for their agonising decision, which unfortunately, at the time of going to press, many months later, has yet to materialise.

In the meantime, I had been searching the internet for any further snippets of interest that might relate to *Kes*. In doing so, I discovered that Ronnie Steele, who had written the book, *Build it for Barry* [73], had also written a companion volume, called *A Blue Plaque for Brian Glover* [74]. I discovered that a blue plaque for Brian Glover had been installed on the walls of Chennells, a bar on Wellington Street in Barnsley, on the 22nd

September 2022. Ken Loach was present at its unveiling, as also was Ronnie Steele and David 'Dai' Bradley. Also present was Brian Glover's son Gus and Brian's widow Tara. Both Ken Loach and Gus Glover performed the unveiling of the plaque. This was very interesting, so I investigated further. Presently, I came across Ronnie's contact details, which was something for which I had been searching for some time but to no avail. So, I promptly fired off an email attaching the latest draft of my book and to ask him if I could use the front cover of *Build it for Barry* for this work. To my delight, Ronnie emailed back. He had no problem with me using the image, so long as I credited the Kes Group and Paul Hilton, their professional photographer. This of course, went without saying.

Ronnie went on to state that some of the images in his book were provided by Barry Hines's first wife Margaret and then asked that if I would like him to ask her permission to use some of these images. This was amazing. Of course, I knew of Margaret through Greg Davies's documentary *Looking for Kes*, but never thought that I might get the opportunity to use any images in her possession. I just couldn't believe it. Ronnie also gave me permission to mention the work of the Kes Group, which I was always proud to do, and even better, Ronnie mentioned its sister group The Kes is Coming Home Group, of which Ronnie was a leader, all I had to do was ask. I was totally unaware of this latter group, so that was a bonus, and if I wanted any information on either group, all I again had to do was ask [75]. And all this even though Ronnie was away on holiday. Aren't *Kes* fans just the greatest? Of course, I answered Ronnie's very encouraging email almost immediately and thanked him for taking time out for my requests. By return, Ronnie's answer was staggering. Margaret Hines had given me full permission to use an image of Barry Hines and David 'Dai' Bradley, together with two kestrels, taken during the filming of *Kes*. This was like the answer to a prayer, for this image was integral for this book. I really needed an image of Barry Hines and David 'Dai' Bradley and without it, I felt my work would be all the poorer. For me, it is the most important image in the book.

Ronnie then emailed back with even more valuable information. Ronnie had been very instrumental in raising the cash for the Barry Hines Memorial, now taking pride of place in Barnsley town centre. What I didn't know was that a resin copy also existed, and which was used in the Barry Hines exhibition that had previously been held at Sheffield University. It is now on permanent loan to the Hoyland Library, which now, of course, meant another *Kes* photographic shoot was in the offing. Not that I needed any encouragement to visit this lovely area. In the meantime, Ronnie had contacted Barry's brother, Richard, who in turn contacted me, which I was certainly not expecting and was a wonderful surprise. We had a long conversation via several emails, during which, he gave me special permission to reproduce a filmed interview that he had performed for the unveiling of the replica Kes statue now in the Hoyland Library. Richard also gave me some very useful constructive criticism of *Discovering Kes*, which I found most useful and applied accordingly. With Richard Hines's permission, the filmed interview reads as follows:

FILMED INTERVIEW WITH RICHARD HINES, BARRY'S BROTHER FOR THE UNVEILING OF THE KES STATUE IN HOYLAND LIBRARY

Question 1. Could you introduce yourself and tell us about you and Barry and how he became a writer and wrote Kes?

I'm Richard Hines, Barry's brother, he was 6 years older than me. Sons of a miner, we lived in Tinker Lane in Hoyland Common as lads. There were no books in our house, except cowboy books by Zane Grey our dad's favourite author. Barry didn't study literature at Ecclesfield Grammar School or Loughborough PE College – football and athletics were his thing. Then one rainy day, stuck in his digs, at college he asked his roommate, Dave Crane, who was studying English Literature if he had anything he could read. Dave lent him a George Orwell's book, *Animal Farm*. This started his passion for reading and gave him the idea to be a writer.

When he married Margaret, they lived a few hundred yards up from Tinker Lane on Hoyland Road. He wrote in a spare bedroom. He didn't have a typewriter and wrote by hand in a school exercise book using a pencil. That's where he wrote his first novel *The Blinder* and *A Kestrel for a Knave,* which was later filmed as *Kes.*

Barry was a grammar schoolboy. I failed my 11-plus exam and ended up at Kirk Balk Secondary Modern. After I'd left school, I took a kestrel I called Kes from a nest in the ruins of Tankersley Old Hall which I kept in a Second World War air raid shelter in Barry and Margaret's garden. One day when I came back from flying my kestrel to the lure in the field behind his house, Barry walked down the garden and told me he was going to write a book about a lad who trains a kestrel.

I was hawk obsessed and loved my kestrel but couldn't see how anybody else would be interested in such a story. I didn't say so. But I told him falconers didn't like kestrels because they were no good for hunting and said to him, 'I wouldn't give him a kestrel if I was thee. I'd give him a goshawk to train'.

It's a good job he didn't take any notice of me!

*****

Question 2: Did you help with the parts of his *A Kestrel for a Knave* which were about falconry?

When he was writing his book, he used to come out each evening with a note pad, and make notes as I weighed, flew, and fed my kestrel.

We used to go for walks on Saturday mornings and Barry asked me about my falconry experiences – which he later used in his book and the film. I told him how I went to Barnsley Library and found a book about Falconry, M. H. Woodford's *A Manual of Falconry*. And how I wasn't allowed to take it out because it was a reference copy – I went to a shop to buy it – unlike Billy Casper, I didn't steal it. I ordered a copy then went back to the library and copied sections out by hand to read while I waited for the book to arrive. There were no photocopiers back then.

One morning I took Barry on the route I had taken to fetch my kestrel and I told him about that. I went with a lad called John Grayson who lived in Hoyland. We went late at night when the farmer would be asleep, carrying a ladder to climb up to the kestrel's nest in Tankersley Old Hall. In Bell Ground Wood John struck up a conversation with a hooting Tawny owl – Barry included this in his novel, but it wasn't included in the film. We came out of the wood into the moonlight, then clambered over the wall and put the ladder against the wall to climb up to the nest to get our kestrels. In the film David Bradley climbed the wall at the Old Hall using climbing pegs hammered into the wall.

*****

Question 3. Can you tell us about being the falconer on the film *Kes*.

In the summer of 1968, I was delighted when Barry got me the job of falconer on the film, training the three kestrels used in the film, and teaching David Bradley, who played Billy Casper, how to fly a kestrel to the glove and lure. All the hawks responded when calling 'Come on Kes', but I gave them individual names. I got the idea from a story my dad told me. At the pit where he worked three friends who were always together, walked into the canteen and a man shouted: 'Here they come – Freeman, Hardy and Willis'. It was the name of a shoe shop, and it amused me and that's what I named the three kestrels.

David Bradley was just 15, I think. He was a lovely lad, and I was full of admiration for him – he worked so hard. After filming all day, he would arrive in a taxi at Barry's house in the evening for his falconry lessons and I would take him into the field to fly the kestrels. Then later he'd go home in a taxi to learn his lines for next day.

David found it difficult flying the kestrels. He said, 'It was 10 times the hardest thing he'd ever done, I was stressed out'. It was my job was to make him into a good falconer, if he wasn't good at it the film wouldn't work – his character needed to be an expert falconer. But he persevered and, in the end, he got really good at lure swinging.

I remember one funny incident. After we'd watched the rushes in the ABC cinema in Barnsley – the film shot that day for the crew to check. I was walking through the town with Barry and Tony Garnett the producer. Barry and me had enjoyed the rushes and were laughing at the swearing and the Barnsley dialect. But Tony had a face like thunder. When Barry asked what was wrong, Tony said, 'We'll end up with an X rated film that won't be understood five miles outside of Barnsley'.

*****

Question 4. Can you tell us how Billy Casper finding the dead hawk in the dustbin was filmed?

The day before filming, the film's props department gave me a frozen dead kestrel they had got from a museum taxidermy department. I thawed it out in our shed and put on its legs a pair of leather jesses – straps used to hold the hawk. Ken Loach's way of getting convincing performances from actors was ruthless. Next day he told me and Freddie Fletcher, who played Billy's bullying brother, to stand next to David Bradley in the dinner queue at the catering van. We did, and Ken came up to me and said, 'Richard, after you've had lunch take Jud to kill the hawk'. David looked at us but didn't say anything. After lunch, making sure he saw us, we walked off.

Later, I was holding the dead kestrel under my jacket when Ken told me to put it in the bottom bin while he distracted David. When the sound and camera were running, Ken told David to run down the garden, feel in the first bin, then the second bin, where poor old David, shocked, took the dead kestrel from the bin.

I'd put the kestrel Jud was supposed to kill on a perch in a spare bedroom at Barry's house and took David there. When I walked down the stairs with it on my glove, David, who was standing in the hall, said, '*I knew you hadn't killed it and Ken was trying to make me roar!!*'.

*****

Question 5: Why did Barry write *Kes*?

On one of our walks, he'd told me he wanted to write *Kes* to '*give the education system some stick*', when at that time the majority of kids were written off at the age of eleven and dumped in secondary modern schools.

It was his skill as a writer, perhaps intuitively, to realise his story of a boy who discovers a talent for something he's good at, flying a soaring hawk, was a metaphor for how family circumstances and a divisive education system, can destroy young people's potential.

Barry had the Yorkshire knack of telling stories, and his work was rooted in his experiences and the stories of Hoyland Common and gave a voice to working-class people and his authenticity and writing skills meant his work not only spoke to people here, but people around the world. *A Kestrel for a Knave* sold over a million copies, became a Penguin Modern Classic and was translated into many languages from German to Japanese, and is on the school curriculum in Australia.

I'm full of admiration for Barry and would like to thank Ronnie Steele and the Kes Group who raised the money for the Barnsley statue, and the Bring Kes Home Group for arranging for the Kes/Billy Casper replica statue to be kept in Hoyland Library on permanent loan, for which I am sure, Barry himself would really have given it his full appreciation.

134

136

[57] The Western Bank Library which houses the Barry Hines Collection. [58] Professor David Forrest (right) signs the author's copy of *Barry Hines, Kes, Threads and Beyond*. [59] The author with the Special Collections archive assistant, Eleanor Mulkeen-Parker (right), in the Western Bank Library. [60] The author examining the first handwritten draft of *A Kestrel for a Knave*. [61] Barry Hine's scarf which was knitted for him by an aunt. [62] Theatre programme from the Nottingham Playhouse production of *Kes*. [63] Chris Miller flies his kestrel for Kenneth Alan Taylor for the Nottingham Playhouse production of *Kes* in May 1984 (courtesy of Chris Miller). [64] Barry Hine's former home in Fulwood Road. [65] The house in Rugby Road, West Bridgford, Nottingham where Barry Hines lived with his partner, Jean Penchion, in 1975. [66] The *Kes* mural at the Arts Tower. [67] John Bishop Murray with one of his very first kestrels (courtesy of John Bishop Murray). [68] John Bishop Murray with the author's male golden eagle, Star. [69] The snooker room at the Hoyland Common Working Men's Club. [70 & 71] *Kes* related posters adorn the wall and stage backdrop of the Hoyland Common Working Men's Club. [72] The footpath leading to Bell Ground Wood where Billy Casper searches for Kes. [73] Cover of the Ronnie Steele book *Build it for Barry* (courtesy of the Kes Group and Paul Hilton). [74] Cover, featuring artwork by Neil Richardson, of Ronnie Steele's second book *A Blue Plaque for Brian Glover* (courtesy of Ronnie Steele). [75] Fred Fletcher (right) with Ronnie Steele (left). Fred made £7,000 in just one fundraising event for the Barry Hines Memorial (courtesy of Ronnie Steele).

Chapter 8

A Blue Plaque for Brian Glover &
A Shock at Barry Hine's Grave
(18th April 2023)

Returning home from the Special Collections Department at Sheffield University, I began to look closely at the documents that I had photographed. Now that I had more time to scrutinise the images, I discovered some previously unknown information that led me to begin thinking about another visit to South Yorkshire. So again, I began to prepare a shoot list which ran as follows:

Hoyland Common

1. Another Barry Hines former home: 124 Hoyland Road, Hoyland Common. This property is where I believe *A Kestrel for a Knave* was written (S74 9NL).

2. Another Barry Hines former home: 32 Tankersley Lane, Hoyland Common (S74 0DS).

3. Hoyland Library, High Croft, Hoyland (S74 9AF).

4. Resin replica of the Barry Hines Memorial, Hoyland Library, High Croft, Hoyland (S74 9AF).

5. Field behind 124 Hoyland Road, Hoyland Common which is where some of the kestrel training and flying took place (S74 9NL).

6. The small park between 78 and 124 Hoyland Road, Hoyland Common, where a new Barry Hines Memorial is planned to be situated.

Barnsley

7. The Brian Glover blue plaque, Chennells, 1 Wellington Street, Barnsley (S70 1SS).

8. Bridge Street, off Old Mill Lane, Barnsley, to photograph the corner that Billy Casper ran round before disappearing through the alley where he picked up the cigarette packet (S71 1PW). As aforementioned, this was apparently not the scene used in Kes. This was Honeywell Street, a parallel street which existed lower down but no longer exists as it did in *Kes* because much of the 1968 housing of the time was demolished during the 1970s.

9. Honeywell Street, the real location of 'Fag Packet Alley'? (S71 1PU).

1. The Queens Hotel, Regent Street, Barnsley, where the cast and crew members used to meet up when filming *Kes* and auditions for the film had taken place (S70 2HP).

2. Ronnie Steele with the author at Chennells, 1 Wellington Street, Barnsley.

3. Ronnie Steele with the author at The Barry Hines Memorial, Cheapside, Barnsley.

In the interim, I had arranged to meet up personally with Ronnie Steele, author of *Build it for Barry* and *A Blue Plaque for Brian Glover*, in the town centre of Barnsley. We set the date of the 18th April 2023 to meet up at the Wetherspoons pub and restaurant on Market Street. As normal, my son David and I set off early in the morning up the M1 motorway and headed for junction 36, where we turned off for Hoyland Common. We had by now become quite familiar with the area, so didn't need the satnav. We parked up outside the former Caspers Fish & Chips shop, where we noticed that no changes had been made since our last visit. All the signage was still in place, which was good news and for the first time, I noticed that the main signboard had been signed by David 'Dai' Bradley. I was surprised I hadn't noticed this before. Then, a thought struck me. For some time, I had been considering the feasibility of a Barry Hines Heritage Centre set up somewhere in either Barnsley or Hoyland Common. Would the building that was once Caspers Fish & Chips shop be a suitable venue? If not, then perhaps a space in Hoyland Library, or somewhere in Barnsley. It could feature possible artifacts, photographs, books etc., but it would need to be open to the public and, I feel, that due to *A Kestrel for a Knave* being Barry's most famous and successful of his nine published novels, it should feature a strong *Kes* theme. Other well-known authors have such centres covering their lives and work, such as the D. H. Lawrence centre at Eastwood, Nottinghamshire, and the Bronte's at Haworth, near Bradford in West Yorkshire, to mention but two, so why not one for Barry Hines? It may amount to nothing but watch this space.

Leaving the car, we headed up Princess Street and out onto Hoyland Road. We bypassed Barry Hines's former home at No. 78, which bore the blue plaque, to seek out the proposed site for the new *Kes* memorial. We had an image taken from the internet to guide us and we soon found it, on the opposite side of the road from No. 78, just a few yards further on [76]. It was easily identifiable due to a glass-covered bus stop and a large stone, emblazoned upon which were the words, 'Hoyland Common'. It is a small, but very pleasant grassy area, although it was plainly obvious that the statue had yet to be erected on this spot. I took a few photographs and then moved on further up Hoyland Road for the next location.

This was No. 124 Hoyland Road, another former residence of Barry Hines [77]. A short walk brought us to the property, which was very impressive, being a large, detached building, which was situated alongside the main Kes flying field, which we had visited on a previous occasion [78]. We had driven past this very house back then, but of course, I had no knowledge of its existence at that time. I only became aware of this property due to our visit to Sheffield University in January 2023. I was particularly interested in this house because, according to a letter in The Barry Hines Archives, Barry was living here in 1968 and 1969. Therefore, there was a strong possibility that this was the house where Barry wrote *A Kestrel for a Knave*, or at least parts of it. It was quite irksome at times during my *Discovering Kes* quest because I was doing this research virtually on my own, with few contact details for anyone who would, as they say, be in the know and be able to advise me. I desired to be as accurate as possible, but sometimes, I knew I would have to make educated guesses, and this was just one instance of several. Did Barry write *A Kestrel for a Knave* at No. 124 Hoyland Road? At this moment in time, I was not 100% certain, but I believe this to be a strong advocate. Some time after submitting *Discovering Kes* for publication, I re-read *A Kestrel for a Knave* and noticed something I had previously missed. On page 104 of the latter, when Mr. Farthing is asking Billy Casper about flying Kes, I noted the following:

"Do you fly it at home?"

"Yes sir, in t' fields at t'back of our house."

"That's Woods Avenue isn't it?"

"Yes sir, 124."

Did Barry use the number 124 deliberately, for he was actually living at No. 124 Hoyland Road, or was it purely coincidental? I, of course, have no means of knowing for certain, but I would put money on it being deliberate, for why else would he select that particular number? I believe it to be further evidence that he was living at this address on Hoyland Road at the time he wrote *A Kestrel for a Knave.*

We wandered further along the road and onto Hawshaw Lane, taking pictures of the flying field along the way until we came to St. Peter's Church and the main footpath to the flying field. I took better images of the church but had to go around the back due to the bright sunlight causing flare from the front. Once this had been accomplished, we set off back towards Caspers where we had parked the car and was surprised to see that the massive EVRi warehouse was highly visible even from this distance. What a blot on the landscape this warehouse surely is.

On arrival back at the car, we then drove on to Tankersley Lane, where we sought out No. 32, another former, and I believe, the final home of Barry Hines. Like No. 124 Hoyland Road, I discovered this information from a document at Sheffield University which stated that Barry was living here in 2014. Two years later, he had sadly passed away, so I imagine that this was his last residence. We found the property easily enough for it was situated just a short distance along the lane. It was a very nice, stone built semi-detached house in a very pleasant location. A few minutes later, with the shots in hand, we set off for Barnsley and our rendezvous with Ronnie Steele. Again, I took the back road through Birdwell and was just approaching the outskirts of Barnsley, when I said to David, "You know what we have forgotten don't you?'

"No, what?" he replied.

"Well, we have forgotten to photograph the replica Kes/Barry Hines Memorial statue in Hoyland library."

How could I have been so stupid as to forget this? It was high on my shoot list for the day. It was too late to do anything about it now because it would have made us too late for our meeting with Ronnie, so I decided that as soon as our Barnsley shoot was complete, we would have to return to Hoyland to include it on my list, if we still had enough time left, that is.

Arriving in Barnsley, we parked up in the Alhambra Shopping Centre as usual and made our way out onto Cheapside, where we again admired the Barry Hines memorial. As we were about half an hour too early, we wandered onto Market Street and visited The Book Vault bookshop, where I enquired if they had a copy of Ronnie Steele's new book, *A Blue Plaque for Brian Glover* available [79]. Fortunately, they had, so I purchased a copy, which was again signed by Ronnie. As aforementioned, we had prearranged to meet Ronnie at the Wetherspoons on Market Street, so we made our way there, ordered two coffees and sat down at a table to await Ronnie's arrival. I had desired to meet Ronnie for some considerable time and now the hour was nigh, I was becoming quite excited. I hoped I had picked the right Wetherspoons, for there are two in Barnsley, although Ronnie did say the one that was only fifty yards or so from the Albert Street café that we had used on a previous visit. Eleven-thirty came and went, and I began to worry a bit. To add to the confusion, although we had never met, I had a basic idea of Ronnie's features because I had seen several images of him. However, I was not exactly certain, so when several Ronnie lookalikes, or doppelgangers, wandered in to the Wetherspoons, we began to worry a bit. We couldn't really ask all of them if they were Ronnie Steele! Fortunately, Ronnie and I had swapped mobile phone numbers, so after about ten minutes or so, I gave him a call. He was very apologetic and told me that he had only just arrived back from a trip to Liverpool and said he would be with us in 10 minutes. Ronnie was true to his word and about 10 minutes later, he walked through the door. We liked him immediately, so down to earth and a genuine person. Over coffees, we then began a wonderful discussion, where I learnt a great deal. I had taken my laptop and showed him sections of my *Kes* talk and we talked at length about the film and its background and about his sterling work arranging memorials and blue plaques, for which I think he deserves an award, particularly after informing us how difficult the process had been, especially with the local council blocking his almost every move. What is it with some councils? At one point, we discussed the BBC documentary *Looking for Kes*, and Ronnie informed me that Greg Davies had interviewed him for one and a half hours for this programme and as such, Ronnie had told his friends that he was going to be appearing in this fine documentary. However, when it was screened, Ronnie's piece had been dropped, which naturally embarrassed Ronnie somewhat. It transpired that the documentary had to be kept to a certain length apparently and the producers already had more than enough material. What a shame, I would have loved to have seen Ronnie's input. I wondered if this was why Barry Hines's grave had not been filmed either, or if it had, had the finished footage also been cut from the final edit? Who knows? Before we moved off to photograph various items on my list, Ronnie presented me with two signed and free copies of both of his lovely books, and in return, I gave him a signed copy of my 'eagle falconry' book.

After about an hour or so, we decided to go out and fulfil the rest of my shoot list in the town and first up was the Brian Glover blue plaque. I had been reading about this in the book that I had just purchased whilst waiting for Ronnie, so had gleaned some information already. It was only a short walk from the Wetherspoons to No. 1 Wellington Street and Chennells [80]. There, the blue plaque [81] was highly prominent, and I took photographs of it and David took several images of Ronnie and myself posing beneath the plaque. It was a memorable moment, and all the time Ronnie was telling us details of how it all came about. Ronnie originally wanted to place the blue plaque on the walls of the Civic Hall, where Brian Glover used to wrestle professionally, but the council wouldn't hear of it. When Ronnie protested, the council said it was a listed building, but, as Ronnie pointed out, there was already a blue plaque to that wonderful Barnsley comedian, the late Charlie Williams on the wall at this site, so why not one for Brian? Ronnie was then informed that Charlie's blue plaque was positioned there without the council's permission. One would have thought that the council would have been proud to extoll the virtues of its famous citizens from the highest rooftops, but not a bit of it, or so it would appear. How shameful is that? Rather surprisingly, Brian's first wife was also none too keen on the idea, but her daughter, Maxine was more in favour. There were other problems too, but Ronnie changed tack and decided to ask the manager at Chennells, where Brian had once done a documentary about his beloved Barnsley, and here the request was much more successful. In fact, the owners, Amber Brewery, were all for the idea and even offered financial help. The plaque was mounted on the outside of the bar and several special people were invited. Ken Loach and Brian's son, Gus Glover officiated by unveiling the plaque and even David 'Dai' Bradley appeared, who now lives not far away in Barnsley. Ronnie informed me that when Ken Loach walked in, the brewery, as soon as they realised Ken was involved, waived their fee, so enamoured were they with this famous film director. How amazing. Music and food were flowing, and Barnsley marketplace was thronged with hundreds of interested people. In all, it was a momentous occasion and yet again, I wished that I could have been involved, but as Ronnie informed me, most of the advertising for the event was local and therefore would have been unlikely to reach Nottingham and at that time, I hadn't yet contacted Ronnie.

Leaving Brian's blue plaque, we then headed for the Barry Hines Memorial on Cheapside, where David took photographs of Ronnie and myself standing beside the statue. The first time we visited the memorial I had noticed a couple of stains on the plinth which were slightly darker than the rest of the stone. I thought this might be natural colouring but decided to ask Ronnie about it. Ronnie's answer was not what I was expecting at all. Yes, they were stains right enough, left behind after the cleaners had removed some graffiti, apparently depicting a human phallus! Why on earth would anyone wish to denigrate such a marvellous monument to such a gifted man? It beggars belief. One could so easily lose one's faith in humanity at times.

After this disturbing news, we headed for Regent Street, passing the Old Civic Hall which had, of course, provided the library in *Kes*. I was so pleased that I had previously photographed this lovely, ornate building, because had it been on my list for this specific visit, I would have been very disappointed, for the entire façade was completely screened off from view from top to bottom with tarpaulin sheets. It was undergoing some serious restoration work by the look of it.

From here, it was but a short walk along Eldon Street to Regent Street, where I photographed the beautiful former Queens Hotel [82]. This is where most of the auditions for *Kes* were held, so it was an important building regarding the *Kes* story and thus had to be included here. In fact, the final auditions for the part of Billy Casper took place here. From 200 initial young hopefuls from 3 different schools, just 30 young lads were trimmed down to around 5 individuals. From these 5, after much deliberation and agonising, David 'Dai' Bradley was finally selected, and what a great choice that was. Ronnie informed me that many famous people, who were performing in Barnsley, would stay here throughout their duration. I had seen this hotel mentioned on several of the *Kes* call sheets held at the Barry Hines Archives, so it was a very useful addition to my *Kes* image library.

Once the hotel had been photographed, we then headed for Bridge Street, where I desired to photograph the end corner of the street where Billy Casper runs round the corner and straight into 'Fag Packet Alley'. Or so I believed. However, Ronnie had informed me that he didn't believe Bridge Street was the correct film location. According to Ronnie, it was Honeywell Street, which runs parallel to Bridge Street but is situated one street further down the hill. So, we went instead to Honeywell Street. The old houses on Honeywell Street were demolished during the 1970s and accordingly the scene looks very different today. Ronnie showed us where he thought the location had previously existed, where there was once a square, now long gone and with a good view over the valley, including a distant school which was there at the time of filming and is still there today. The old Salt Paper Mill has now apparently been replaced by an Asda superstore. I have to admit that it was not easy to imagine the scene back then, but I still took several photographs for posterity. Even though this was no doubt the scene, and Ronnie was right, I planned to use these images, along with the one's I already had of Bridge Street, the latter purely to demonstrate what the area would have looked like in 1968. Ronnie told us that at one stage, Brian Glover lived in a bungalow on Honeywell Street, which is apparently still there. These two streets had posed yet another anomaly. Which was the real site for 'Fag Packet Alley'? I needed to be sure, otherwise, later, I am sure someone would take delight in correcting me, so upon my return home, I compared images taken as screen grabs from the film with my images taken on Bridge Street and expanded them on my computer to show detail. This was not to doubt Ronnie in the slightest, but he did say at one point that he was not 100% certain that Honeywell Street was the real film location. However, Ronnie appeared to be right, for although the brickwork and flooring of the alley on Bridge Street was very, very similar, it did not appear quite the same as that in the original film footage. So, from this it appears that Honeywell Street was the right location well enough, but it had unfortunately changed beyond all recognition since 1968. I finally decided that I would use images of both sites as the one on Bridge Street still visibly demonstrated how the scene appeared back then.

Another anomaly that Ronnie cleared up for me concerned the St. Helen's Primary School at Monk Bretton which I had photographed on the 19th January 2022. I previously thought that this school was on the same ground as that used for *Kes*, but apparently, this isn't so. The St. Helen's Secondary Modern school that was used for *Kes* was apparently on Carlton Road, Athersley South, where today the Holy Trinity School campus is now situated. So, that was another unexpected revelation. This is what comes of researching on one's own without valuable outside knowledgeable assistance, as I had been doing for the past two years, and then the pleasure of suddenly being helped by someone who went to schools in this area, so Ronnie would be in the most favourable position of anyone I knew personally who would know of such facts. Ronnie, who was a very keen footballer, had actually played professional football and even played on the original *Kes* football field.

Ronnie also cleared up another small mystery for me. I had read, I think somewhere on the internet, that Barry Hines's funeral service was held at St. Paul's church at Pilley which is not far from Tankersley. Ronnie, who had read an eulogy for Barry at his funeral was, again, in a real position to know the correct location for sure, so I asked him. The account of the site at Pilley was untrue. Barry's funeral, as I originally believed, was indeed at St. Peter's church at Tankersley. I was truly grateful to Ronnie for clarifying this information. The last thing I needed was to include any wrong locations or incorrect information if possible. This was precisely why I was cross checking everything where there could possibly be some doubt. However, having said that, any inaccuracies are entirely mine.

So, after these very useful revelations, we made our way back into the town centre where Ronnie then collected his car, and we went our own way, back to the Alhambra and then headed south again to find Hoyland Library. We drifted into Hoyland and soon found a small car park across the road from a large building. This was the Hoyland Centre, which at first, we didn't recognise as the library, but upon closer inspection, we discovered that the building, apart from housing the library, also had other uses **[83]**. It was a GP surgery, an NHS community service, and a pharmacy. We entered the building and almost immediately caught sight of the replica Kes statue, and we lost no time in photographing it **[84]**. It was almost identical to the bronze statue in Cheapside, but this one was made of resin. Although it really did look identical in both size and colouration, tapping it with my fingernails demonstrated that it was light and hollow and not made of metal. Even so, it was a very imposing piece and would look very nice in my living room

I have to say! There were two brass plaques affixed to its pedestal. The upper one reads [85]:

```
Provided By
The Extensive Work Of The
Barnsley
Kes Group
And The Hoyland
Kes Is Coming Home Group
```

And the lower plaque reads [86]:

```
This Sculpture Is Dedicated To
BARRY HINES
1939 - 2016
A Great Writer
An Inspiring Teacher
A True Working Class Hero
Sculptor – Graham Ibbeson
```

After securing some images of the statue, we still had time enough to revisit Tankersley Old Hall, where we discovered that the rickety old stile had been renovated and the surrounding overgrown vegetation had been cleared. David discovered a piece of the old stile lying beneath the surrounding vegetation, so we took it home as a souvenir. Well, it would only have rotted had we left it *in-situ*. We decided to take an image of myself imitating Billy Casper, by standing on the woodland side of the stile, looking towards the old hall with a blade of grass hanging from my mouth, just as David 'Dai' Bradley, as Billy Casper had done more than half a century ago. At the same time, and at long last, just as we were taking these photographs, a hovering kestrel came into view less than 100 yards away. It then flew off over Tankersley Old Hall. This was very auspicious and the very first time that we had seen a kestrel in the vicinity of the old hall, and it almost certainly would have been a descendent of the original pair that occupied the hall in 1968. What a pleasant surprise that turned out to be. I understand that kestrels still nest in Tankersley Old Hall but apparently now breeding on the inside of the inner walls, as the outer walls now hold few, if any suitable nesting crevices. Long may they continue to do so.

One last port of call was our usual visit to Barry Hines's grave in St. Peter's churchyard, but unbeknown to us, we were in for a bit of a shock. We took our cameras and flask of coffee to sit in mild contemplation for a while on one of the two benches close beside Barry's grave, as it was a lovely, warm, sunny afternoon. We had done a lot of walking during the day, and we were beginning to feel the effects, and decided on a spite of rest for half an hour or so before setting off back home to Nottingham.

However, as we approached the grave, we noticed immediately that something wasn't right. Of course, we knew exactly where the grave was, for we had visited it on numerous occasions, but something was missing. At first, as daft as it sounds, we couldn't locate the grave because the headstone had vanished. We always looked for the headstone, but this time, it simply wasn't there, and as such, the scene looked very different from normal. We knew we were at the right spot, but the grave had been dug over and was mounded above the surrounding grass. We just looked at each other and wondered what on earth was going on. Had someone stolen the headstone? Surely not. Then it all became crystal clear. A short length of timber, about three or four inches wide, had been inserted, not at the head end, but at the lower end of the grave, which is why we missed it at first. Then I took a closer look at this piece of wood and found the words written upon its length in felt-tip indelible ink: Hines/Mulvey.

"Oh my God," I uttered to David.

"It looks like Eleanor Mulvey, Barry's second wife has recently passed away and was now sharing Barry's grave."

We couldn't believe it and we both felt somewhat sick to the pit of our stomachs. Now it was obvious as to why the headstone had been removed. It had no doubt been taken away to the stonemasons for further engraving, whereby adding Eleanor's details upon it. I had no idea that Eleanor had sadly passed away, very recently too by the look of it. In fact, we had only been talking about her with Ronnie that very morning. How coincidental was that? We were both literally stunned, for we could never have imagined this in our wildest dreams. We had even photographed one of the houses she had shared with Barry that very morning, namely, 32 Tankersley Lane. This was weird to say the least. We photographed the now rearranged grave and then sat on the bench to have our coffee, still in utter disbelief. It had spoilt the day to some extent. I had never met Eleanor and only knew of her from *Looking for Kes*, but even so, it was a twist in the tale that was most unexpected. We sat on the bench for at least half an hour, contemplating, before finally saying our goodbyes and headed for our car and the M1. We pulled into Woodall services on the M1 for another coffee at Starbuck's and from there I sent off a text to Ronnie Steele. I was almost certain that he was unaware of Eleanor's demise as he would surely have mentioned it, especially as we were earlier that very morning discussing her. On arrival home, I sent Ronnie a selection of the images we had taken during the day, including shots of the now temporarily disarranged grave. I then checked on the internet to detect if anything had been entered about Eleanor, but oddly, there was nothing concerning her passing. This was yet another surprise in my quest to discover aspects of *Kes*. I emailed David Forrest at Sheffield University with the news, and he informed me that he too had only just heard about Eleanor's passing. She had apparently died from dementia, similarly to her late husband. How tragic.

147

It was at this stage that I decided that I had one more excursion to Barnsley still to undertake. Ever since Ronnie Steele had informed me that St. Helen's Primary School was not the correct location for *Kes*, I was niggled that this part had not been successfully completed and I could not finish this account by leaving this oversight unremedied. Additionally, Ronnie had sent me an image of the rear of 'the *Kes* House', at 56 Parkside Road. I didn't know that this area was accessible, so I desired to view this for myself. I also required more images of Skiers Spring Colliery from further along from the main Broad Carr Road. Obviously, another trip had now to be arranged.

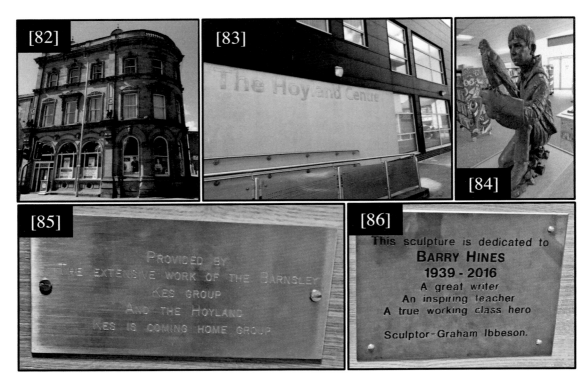

[76] Marker stone for Hoyland Common at the site for the proposed *Kes*/Barry Hines memorial statue. [77] Barry Hines's house in Hoyland Road, Hoyland Common. He was resident here in 1968 at which time he wrote *A Kestrel for a Knave*. [78] Barry Hine's former home in Tankersley Lane, Hoyland Common. [79] Ronnie Steele holding a copy of his Brian Glover book. [80] Chennells in Barnsley. [81] The Brian Glover blue plaque at Chennells. [82] The former Queens Hotel in Regent Street where many of the auditions for *Kes* were held. [83] The Hoyland Centre (Hoyland Library) where the replica Barry Hines Memorial is on permanent loan from the Kes Group and the Kes is Coming Home Group. [84] The replica Barry Hines Memorial statue. [85 & 86] Inscriptions on the replica Barry Hines Memorial statue.

Chapter 9

Billy Casper's School, Skier's Spring Colliery & 'Fag Packet Alley' (25ᵗʰ May 2023)

This excursion was planned to be the final shoot for this book. Future research will no doubt turn up more locations and *Kes* facts, but I had to draw the line somewhere, otherwise this book would never have seen the light of day.

1. Trinity School Campus, Carlton Road, Athersley South, Barnsley. The site of the original school where Kes was filmed in 1968 (S71 2LF).

2. The '*Kes* House' 56 Parkside Road, Hoyland Common. I planned to inspect and photograph the rear of this property. It was here that the mews for *Kes* was built and nearby was where the catering vehicle for the cast and crew was situated (S74 0AH).

3. A closer look at the site of Skier's Spring Colliery, Jud's workplace in *Kes* (S74 9BU).

4. The correct film location for 'Fag Packet Alley', which was apparently down John Edward Street, and into Sarah Ann Street and back up into Honeywell Street.

5. Brian Glover's former home on Honeywell Street.

Before setting off for this latest jaunt, I needed to be clear in my mind as to the actual location of 'Fag Packet Alley'. I was very aware of making unnecessary errors and after talking with Ronnie Steele, I was even more confused. I needed to get everything as near perfect as possible, but this location was causing such a problem that I began losing sleep over it. Which was the correct location, Bridge Street or Honeywell Street? I began by rechecking all my sources, including David 'Dai' Bradley's website, which I had not viewed for quite some time. I was trying to work out as to where I originally found the idea that 'Fag Packet Alley', was on Bridge Street, and here it was, on his paper round section, and I quote: 'Returning to the Newsagents he dashes into Bridge Street off Old Mill Lane (the pyjama kid's terraces are now bungalows) and through one of the arches-picking up an empty fag packet.'

Yet Ronnie was convinced that this was not the location, so I forwarded the relevant portion of the website to Ronnie for his comments. Unbeknown to me, Ronnie was unfortunately in hospital recovering from an operation, so it was even more amazing that he replied almost by return.

From his hospital bed, Ronnie made some enquiries and in his replying email, he told me that everyone he contacted had said for certain that the street(s) in the film were, at one time, off Honeywell Street. A lifetime trusted friend of Ronnie's, a man named Bob, sent Ronnie the following details: 'It was off Honeywell Street opposite Honeywell pub. Go down the street, turn left at the bottom, carry on down the ginnel[1] on the right, looking towards Keel Field, named after Keel Inn. If you carried on past the ginnel at the bottom of John Edward Street, you turn into Sarah Ann Street which took you back onto Honeywell Street'.

Ronnie stated that if I was to follow this description, it would show that John Edward Street and Sarah Ann Street were, in effect, an avenue. The sequence of the film though, shows Casper first of all running down Sarah Ann Street and turning right (not left) at the bottom.

Well, Ronnie could not be more clear or concise than this, so this section of the website is likely incorrect. This demonstrates that when researching such documents, it pays to check and double check all accounts whenever possible. So, yet again, I had good cause to be grateful to Ronnie Steele.

Early on the 25th May 2023, my son David and I set off yet again to fulfil yet another photographic shoot. At the top of my list was the Holy Trinity School at Athersley South, Barnsley. This was very important to me for so much of *Kes* was filmed here. Although the original St. Helen's Secondary School on this site had long been demolished, and then replaced by the Edward Sheerien School, which also had been demolished, the current school on this site was only opened in 2012 and is a coeducational all-through school for pupils aged 3 (nursery) to 16.

Driving through Barnsley centre, we soon located the Holy Trinity School on Carlton Road, Athersley South. After parking in the large car park, we spotted the sign for the school reception and made a beeline for it. The school was much larger than I had anticipated, and the security was evident everywhere. There were cameras mounted on tall posts all over the place and even access to reception was not straightforward. We had to press a wall mounted button, which opened the front door, but access to a second door was not possible until the first door had closed behind us. Only then, were we admitted to the inner sanctum. These doors could also be controlled by the receptionists manning the main desk. All this security is, of course, unfortunately necessary today, all due to a few nutcases carrying firearms and shooting pupils and teachers alike, as well as a seeming plethora of paedophiles. In my day, we never heard of such atrocities, but such have sadly become ever more commonplace. Therefore, it was necessary that we approached the proper channels for our *Kes* quest. Strangers like us, especially armed

---

[1] A ginnel is a word in the Yorkshire dialect describing a fenced or walled alley between residential buildings that provides a pedestrian shortcut to nearby streets. Ginnels are typically found in suburban areas, and contain no business premises, unlike other types of alleys, such as a snicket, another common Yorkshire description, or twitchell, as we call them in Nottingham.

with cameras, are also a definite no-no around young children, especially on school properties, so, an initial approach to reception was vital.

However, the head teacher, we were informed was at a meeting and would be so for quite some time and without some form of official sanction, we would be getting nowhere. Additionally, the school was also filling up with myriad pupils, and I had my big Nikon camera mounted with 400mm zoom lens in full view around my neck. The receptionists phoned somebody who suggested that we should return after school had finished, when no pupils would be around. This made perfect sense, so I left the receptionists with my mobile phone number so that someone in authority could ring me later in the day, and we then left to continue the rest of the days shoot, planning to return to the school after three in the afternoon. To be perfectly truthful, we were expecting a flat refusal to take photographs at the school, and I couldn't really blame them, so our hopes were not high.

Whilst still in Barnsley, we decided to try and discover more about 'Fag Packet Alley', so we first drove up Bridge Street off Old Mill Lane. My purpose here was to pay special attention to the last alley on this street, which I had formerly supposed was the one used in *Kes*. I had previously neglected to photograph anything beyond the alley and ever since had wondered about this oversight. I planned to lay this to rest this very day. We soon found Bridge Street and drove down to the last alley on the right, which I had formerly presumed was the film location. However, this time, I looked beyond the alley and further down the street. Here I noticed that relatively new houses had been built just beyond the old buildings housing the alley. These new houses were set further back than the original ones that they had replaced. Perhaps there had been more alleys present back in 1968. I also searched for the end of the street where Billy Casper runs around the corner and through the alley. The fact that older houses on the right-hand side of Bridge Street stretched further than the old houses on the left, led me to search for the road that once must have been present, if this was the correct location. I found a rather narrow alleyway, but this was positioned opposite the end of the new houses on the left. This made me think that if this alleyway was what I thought it was, then that would mean that there were at one time, more alleys present in the demolished houses, so that also meant that the alley that I photographed previously, would not have been the original alley in any event. Oh boy, this all was becoming rather confusing, but it was going to be more confusing still. Remembering Ronnie Steele's words about Honeywell Street being the real location, we decided to concentrate our efforts in that region, which was only one street away.

We drove down Honeywell Street to the point where we had visited with Ronnie, when he was showing us the view from the new build houses. We spotted a lady in her garden and asked her if she knew where John Edward Street and Sarah Ann Street might be found. It transpired that despite living on Honeywell Street for the past 21 years, she had never heard of either. This was very disappointing. When we informed her as to why we were looking for these streets, because of *Kes*, she became very interested indeed, as most people did when we informed them of our quest. She told us that David 'Dai' Bradley still lived on Honeywell Street and I knew this was factual because Ronnie Steele had previously given me this information. I had never asked for the exact location as I presumed that David might not be particularly interested in me or my book. The lady also told me that David's sister owned a shop at the Old Mill Lane end of Honeywell Street, and I had earlier stood outside this shop taking photographs of the bridge that crossed over Old Mill Lane [87]. At that point, I had no idea that the shop belonged to David's sister. It is amazing how these interesting little facts have emerged during my quest for *Kes*. Even so, we drove up and down Honeywell Street searching for the elusive two streets with no success whatsoever. They didn't even show up on our satnavs. The only conclusion I could reach is that they must have been demolished, for there were numerous new builds in this area. Before leaving Honeywell Street, I decided to attempt to find Brian Glover's former home. Ronnie Steele had informed me that it was a bungalow, so we drove further down the street to find not one, but two semi-detached, white painted bungalows. But which one was Brian Glover's former home? I later sent the resulting image to Ronnie Steele asking him which was which. It transpired that neither of them was correct, his bungalow was next door to these two and not white painted but in original red brick! Ronnie had kindly spoken to the current occupant of the dwelling who confirmed that Brian had indeed lived there formerly. Yet again Ronnie had come to the rescue and even sent me some images of Brian's former home for use in this work [88]. Ronnie, and Professor David Forrest of Sheffield University were both so generous with their time and gave their knowledge so freely to me. I will always be grateful for this kindness. We then decided to leave Barnsley for the time being and head south for Hoyland Common.

My next quest was to discover if we could locate an entrance to the rear of 56 Parkside Road, the house the *Kes* crew used as Billy, Jud, and Mrs. Casper's house. We drove past Caspers Fish & Chips shop to determine if any changes had taken place, but it sadly remained the same as on our previous visits. From there, we drove down Fitzwilliam Street and out onto the Sheffield Road, heading south for a short distance until we came to Parkside Road. Soon we were opposite No. 56, but there was no side entrance visible, so we pushed on a few yards further and came to an entrance which was barred by a green painted gate. David went to check if the gate was unlocked, which it was, so he opened it and I drove through until the driveway opened into a much wider space. In the meantime, David had been speaking to a resident and told him why we were there. He told us the green painted gate had only been erected some three weeks previously and only one key had so far been issued to the residents, which had caused some concern. This resident was a very useful contact, for he showed us exactly where the catering vehicle had been parked [89]. He was living there at the time and remembered it all well. He had met David 'Dai' Bradley and spoke very highly of him. I asked him if the mews was positioned in the same place, but he said no, it was at the opposite end of this lovely little lane, beyond a large conifer in the back garden of No. 56. I had Ronnie Steele's photograph of the catering area on my mobile phone and opened the image to determine if we were in the right place. We were and so I began to take several images. This was great. We then ambled down the track towards the large conifer, noticing a large field on our left, from where we could see Bell Ground Wood in the distance. We were informed that this field was due to be built on, so yet another lovely area of green belt land was about to disappear under bricks and tarmac. What a sad indictment. This was very likely another field where the kestrels for the film could have been trained and flown. The track unfortunately ended at the house next to No. 56, so we could peer no further. We took several more images here and then took our leave for the next item on my shoot list.

Ever since our earlier visits to the Barnsley area, I had desired to pay a somewhat more sustained visit to the region where Skier's Spring Colliery was situated. We set off down Sheffield Road and turned left into Broad Carr Road, following this for a few hundred yards and pulled into the layby where we previously took photographs of a railway bridge crossing above a wide track [90]. I wanted to find, if possible, any traces of the old colliery, but apart from several metal posts marked with the letter B. M. B. C., (Barnsley Metropolitan Borough Council?), the area was now a beautiful section of woodland with many wildflowers in evidence [91]. We wandered through the wood until we came to some fields, one of which contained a couple of horses [92]. No signs of a derelict coal mine though, so after taking numerous photographs, we retraced our steps back to our car and headed back up Sheffield Road, turning down Tankersley Lane to head for St. Peter's Church. We were hoping to discover a newly engraved headstone crowning Barry Hines's grave, but we were to be disappointed. Only the Hines/Mulvey plank of wood remained to inform passers-by that this was the final resting place of this wonderful author. There were no fresh flowers brightening up the grave, so I concluded, rightly or wrongly, that it had been Eleanor Mulvey, Barry's second wife who had been responsible for most, if not all the floral tributes that we had previously noted. No fresh flowers had been added since our last visit over a month previously. As usual, we sat and enjoyed a coffee on the benches close to Barry's grave, mulling over whether a return to Barnsley and the Holy Trinity School would be worth the effort. I have to say, we both had our doubts, but then again, I didn't relish spending the rest of my life wondering, what if? We deduced that at the very worst-case scenario, the school could only say no to our request, so, with hope in our hearts, we decided to make the drive back up to Barnsley.

We arrived back at the school at 2.45pm and decided to wait in the car until the pupils began to leave for home. We still had not received a phone call, which was worrying, so just after 3pm, we decided to walk up the school drive to the reception area. The receptionist that we spoke to during our morning visit, Faye Steel, was still there, but she could not get hold of anyone to give us permission to take photographs. But then, by an immense stroke of luck, Faye attracted the attention of an English teacher, Sonja Walker, who happened to be passing by. She was a lovely lady who immediately became interested in our *Kes* project, and began to take us to the football field, scene of Brian

Glover's epic Manchester United and Tottenham Hotspur 5th round cup tie. I took several images before venturing onto this hallowed ground. The ground was covered with artificial turf, which was very soft to walk upon, and here, I took more images. We couldn't believe that we were now standing on this great piece of cinematic history. I took shots of the school buildings, which of course, were sadly not the same one's that stood here in 1968. All the same it was an impressive looking school and appeared to be built on at least part of the original foundations. I could easily imagine Tibbutt giving his 'V' sign to Mr. Sugden, for the scene was very similar. Either way, this was the actual school scene where much of *Kes* was shot. I was over the moon to be given this great privilege, but even better was yet to come.

Sonja had accompanied us back to reception and I thought that these images were to be the final one's taken for this book. But the day was not yet over. Sonja, bless her, hailed Tony, the caretaker, who was passing us by and asked him if it would be possible to take photographs of the football field from the roof of the school! As Sonja said, that would be quite something, and Tony agreed. I have to say right here and now, nobody, but nobody, is allowed on the school roof. Even Sonja herself, who had taught here for 8 years, had never been on the roof. We had to wait a few minutes for Tony to return from a visit to the school office and he then led us, together with Sonja, through at least two locked gates or doors before we ascended the roof proper. Tony advised us that we would have to remain under his strict supervision and to keep away from the edge of the roof, as a fall would not be a good idea. Once on the rooftop, I was amazed to discover a maze of pipes, central heating systems, ventilation units and other machinery, which made progression across the roof rather awkward, but even so, this was something that I could never have dreamed of and was so grateful. We followed Tony's instructions to the letter and finally made our way to the roof area which overlooked the treasured football field. To obtain such elevated images of this ground was indeed a great privilege, and I took full advantage of this most unexpected opportunity, taking many images from different angles [93]. Oddly enough, we came across a prostrate plastic falcon lying on top of a metal cabinet. How bizarre was that? We were here for *Kes*, a much smaller falcon species, whereas this plastic, bird scaring model, was the size of a female Arctic Gyrfalcon *(Falco rusticolus)* the world's largest falcon. Tony held it whilst I took images of it with him and Sonja, and then I joined them so that David could take an image which included me with these two lovely, very helpful people [94]. Visiting this school at long last was the icing on the cake and I am so grateful for the experience and so relieved that we decided to return to Barnsley to complete this quest. As such, this was an appropriate and fitting episode upon which to finalise this book, and I could not have been happier. I was so pleased that we had made the journey from author Barry Hines's final resting place in Tankersley to the Holy Trinity School. What an adventure this quest had become.

This book has taken well over two years of research, with a total of 8 full day and 2 half day visits to Barnsley, Hoyland Common, Doncaster and Sheffield University. This has now become an area with which I have come to love and have become reasonably familiar with. Although there have been a few disappointments along the way, such as several emails to various people that have remained unanswered, (there could, of course, be perfectly good reasons for the latter). Perhaps the most disappointing of all, was the fact that after 9 months of my initial request to the agency for permission to include the documents that I had photographed at the Sheffield University Archives, no reply, positive or negative, has yet been forthcoming. And this despite an email I sent to the agency five months after my initial request as a reminder, for which I never received a reply and which of course meant that I cannot now use these valuable images for this work, other than the one's taken by my son David, depicting me holding a few of the said artifacts. As these were distant images showing the documents in my hands, whereby no information is discernible, I considered these to be safe enough to not require copyright for use here. Other than this, writing this book has been a real labour of love and I sincerely hope that through the efforts taken, this work may help and encourage other *Kes* fans to follow in my footsteps and perhaps visit some of the film locations described within these pages. I also hope that I have done the film and all those involved in producing the film, some small measure of justice. Additionally, I sincerely hope that this missive helps in some small way to perpetuate the memory of the author Barry Hines and in remembering his most famous work. My research is ongoing, and in time, I fully expect to unearth other interesting facts regarding this incredible story, which, hopefully, will find their way into possible future editions of this work. As I was penning my final words for this book, the occasion of my 75th birthday took place, when I received an amazing birthday card designed by my grandson, Joshua. He used an image of Billy Casper and superimposed an image of my male golden eagle, Star, in place of Kes [95]. I was completely overwhelmed by this gesture, and I thought it made a fitting end to my quest for *Kes*.

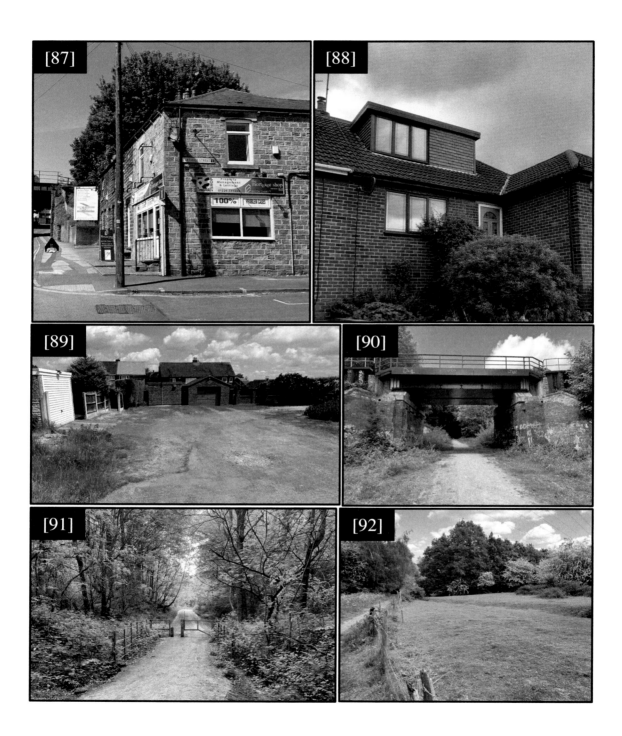

[87] Corner of Bridge Street and Old Mill Lane where David 'Dai' Bradley's sister apparently has a shop. [88] Former home of Brian Glover (courtesy of Ronnie Steele). [89] Area at the back of Parkside Road where the film crew set up their catering vehicle during filming. [90] The railway bridge at the former Skiers Spring Colliery. [91] A track through the woods where the Skiers Spring Colliery once stood. [92] The green landscape which now covers the location of the former Skiers Spring Colliery. [93] The football pitch (now artificial) where the match between 'Manchester United' and 'Tottenham Hotspur' took place in *Kes*. [94] The author (right) with the caretaker (holding a plastic falcon used to deter other birds) and English teacher (Sonja Walker) who was instrumental in arranging for access to the school roof so that photographs of the famous football pitch could be taken. [95] A *Kes* inspired birthday card.

Appendix 1

The Cast of *Kes*

For the benefit of those who have yet to see Kes, the cast of the film is shown below.

Billy Casper (the star of the film) ………………………………David 'Dai' Bradley

Jud Casper (Billy's brother) ………………………….......... Freddie Fletcher

Mrs. Casper (Billy's mother) ………………………………. Lynne Perrie

Mr. Farthing (Billy's English teacher) ………………….......... Colin Welland

Mr. Gryce (Billy's headmaster) …………………………….... Robert 'Bob' Bowes

Mr. Sugden (Billy's PE teacher) …………………………. Brian Glover

Mr. Hesketh (Billy's form teacher) ……………………….... Himself

Youth Employment Officer ………………………………….Bernard Atha

Boy's mother waiting for Youth Employment Officer ………….Mary Southall

Newsagent ………………………………………….... Harry Markham

Butcher ……………………………………………….. Leslie Stringer

Farmer at Monastery Farm ……………………………….… Len Bolderson

Librarian ……………………………………………….. Zoe Sunderland

Lady in betting shop ……………………………………….. Julie Goodyear

Man in betting Shop ……………………………………….. Ted Carroll

Milkman …………………………………………………… Duggie Brown

Floyd (Fish & Chips Shop owner) ………………………….. Bill Dean

Billy's Mum's boyfriend in the Cudworth Hotel ………….......... Joe Miller

Mrs. Casper's friend in the Cudworth Hotel ……………………. Rose MacLean

Jud's friend …………………………………………………. John Grayson

Billy's math's teacher ………………………………………. Geoffrey Banks

Comedian at the Cudworth Hotel ………………………….… Joey Kaye

Backing music at the Cudworth Hotel ……………………….......... 4D Jones Band

MacDowell (Billy's bullying classmate) …………………………. Robert Naylor

Mrs. MacDowell .... Beryl Carroll

Bible reader in assembly .... Jean Palmer

Desmond Guthrie (Billy's classmate) .... Himself

Julie Shakespeare (Girl in Billy's class) .... Herself

Stephen Crossland (Billy's classmate) .... Himself

George Speed (Billy's classmate) .... Himself

Mike Padgett (Billy's classmate) .... Himself

Frank Norton (Billy's classmate) .... Himself

Peter Clegg ('Cleggie') .... Himself

Tibbutt (Billy's classmate) .... David Glover

First year schoolboy who was caned in error .... Martin Harley

Appendix 2

Some Advice for Budding Falconers

This appendix is intended as guidance for the benefit of possible future budding Billy Casper's' regarding falconry.

Some of the Pro's and Con's.

I think it highly unlikely that Barry Hines, Ken Loach, Tony Garnett, or any other member of the *Kes* cast or crew could have foreseen the fact that the film would have influenced some young schoolboys, eager to emulate the film's main star, to venture out into the countryside to take a kestrel illegally for themselves. As I stated earlier, although there were undoubtedly some, I simply do not believe the alleged huge number of kestrels taken, which was claimed by certain conservation bodies, and I have given my reasons for this within this text. Having said this, however, there is no doubt that some youngsters probably began their falconry careers in just this manner. Therefore, I would be mortified if I thought for one moment, the same scenario would occur from reading this book, hence my reasons for penning this section. There is a lot more to falconry than what one might imagine, and it takes a huge amount of patience and time for little reward. Herewith, a plea:

Please, do not, under any circumstances, attempt to take a kestrel, or any other raptor from the wild in the United Kingdom. It is illegal, totally unnecessary, and most likely will result in a heavy fine at the very least, together with a criminal record.

I thought it might be useful to begin by reiterating an event that took place a few years ago when I, along with other members of the British Falconer's Club Eagle Group, had taken our eagles along to place them in a static display arena at the International Centre for Birds of Prey (now closed to the public) at Newent in Gloucestershire. The event was for a falconry weekend, and we had been invited by the owner, Jemima Parry-Jones MBE, to stage part of a two-day event for the public on the involvement of eagles and many other raptor species in falconry and raptor conservation. At one point during the event, I was approached by a person who was interested in becoming a falconer, and he asked me how much, financially, it would cost for him to begin. I began by saying that to do it properly he would be out of pocket by at least £3,000 - £4,000. He was horrified and screeched, "What! I can get a Harris Hawk *(Parabuteo unicinctus)* for about £350, so where did I get **that** figure from?" I informed him that yes, I am sure he could acquire one for that price, but where was he going to keep it and what would he feed it on? I then find out if he planned to fly the hawk at wild quarry.

proceeded to give a breakdown of some of the costs involved. First though, I needed to find out if he planned to fly the hawk at wild quarry. He answered in the affirmative, so I asked if he had permission to fly his hawk over suitable land that held sufficient numbers of quarry species, as that would determine the type of hawk that he wished to fly. Was the land wide open with few trees, such as moorland? If so, he would be perhaps better served with a falcon, or if it was more enclosed with patches of woodland, a goshawk, sparrowhawk, or a Harris hawk would be the raptor of choice. He said he had some parkland where he could exercise it, but it was also visited by members of the public. This of course was of no use whatsoever. Attempting to fly at quarry in a public park would soon cause him, and the noble art of falconry, many problems. I told him he would need good areas of private land, for which he would require permission from the landowner and that could cost him so much per annum, and that was if he could obtain permission in the first place, good land is in very short supply. He obviously hadn't thought this part through at all.

Where was he going to keep the bird? I wanted to know.

"I have a spare bedroom, I plan to keep it in there to begin with," he replied. I told him that this was no good at all. He would need either a large shed, or an outside flight of suitable dimensions and quality. Either of which was very likely to incur a cost of at least £1,000. He also had no idea of the mess that a hawk can make with its mutes (droppings) if kept indoors. With falconry, saving, skimping, and trying to cut corners would, sooner rather than later, cost him dearly, one way or another. My next question concerned food supplies for the bird. He planned to use roadkill and butcher's meat, neither of which was suitable. Roadkill, especially today, is a complete no-no, because although the corpse may well have been freshly killed by a vehicle, there is no way one can be certain that it was not diseased in some way, especially for a beginner with no experience. It is even more dangerous today because of the outbreaks of avian influenza. Also, many wild species may carry an array of parasites of one type or another. Butcher's meat should only be used in the short term. The next piece of advice stunned him even further, when I informed him that falconers today mostly purchased their hawk food ready frozen from commercial suppliers, such as Honeybrook Farm, and it wasn't cheap. He would also need a decent sized chest freezer in which to store the rats, mice, day-old chicks, rabbits, and quail to provide the hawk with a mixed diet. A suitable freezer would perhaps set him back about £300, if not more. So, a batch of food and a freezer would give him little change from around £600. He was beginning to turn somewhat pale, and I hadn't even finished.

I next suggested that he should join a falconry club, preferably the British Falconer's Club and thus attempt to get an experienced mentor there who might be able to guide him properly. Again, he would need to pay a club subscription. Did he know about falconry equipment I asked? It turned out that he didn't know much at all. He kept referring to jessies [96-99]. I corrected him and told him the leather straps around the legs were termed jesses, not jessies. Did he know about radio telemetry? No, he had never heard of it, so I explained about transmitters, receivers, and the latest GPS systems, also explaining that it was a complete fool who flew hawks free without telemetry of one sort or another and added that the cost of such, for a decent set, such as those made by Marshall, would set him back at least another £1,000 **[100]**. I think he was now beginning to understand the reasons why I told him that the total cost would be around £3,000 - £4,000, and this did not include the everyday items, such as hawk baths, hoods, swivels, leashes, gloves, hawking bags or vests, lures, bow perches, ring perches, block perches, weighing scales, good quality leather for making jesses and hoods, travel boxes, falconry books, hood pouches and equipment making tools etc. **[101-105]**. He was now beginning to look somewhat troubled. I also told him that he needed to ask himself how much he really wanted to practice falconry. I thought he was going to faint. I then explained that if he didn't want to make his own equipment, there were now plenty of suppliers selling first class falconry equipment, unlike when I first began when there were no suppliers of equipment whatsoever.

Next there was the important fact of weight control. Basically, a bird at full body weight will be unlikely to fly to the falconer for food, or chase quarry. The smaller the hawk, the less leeway in weight control. With a kestrel for example, we are talking in grams, or fractions of an ounce. The hawk's body fat is also a problem for a beginner. Once the hawk's weight is reduced, the hawk initially relies upon layers of stored body fat. Once this has been absorbed, the hawk's weight will suddenly drop, literally overnight. If this is not spotted, the hawk will soon die, so strict weight management is crucial to success. For a beginner, this is difficult to understand, and that is why beginning with a small hawk, such as a kestrel, is not a good idea. He must learn all about weight control from the start, preferably from an experienced mentor, and this cannot be over emphasised. It is the key to successful falconry, without it, no progress is possible. Therefore, a hawk such as a Harris hawk, or a red-tailed hawk, being much larger than a kestrel, would be the best bet.

Depending on the species, some raptors can live for thirty years or even more, so taking on a bird is not something to be careless about. Being prepared to keep a hawk for such a long period of time was a question that I posed. After all, a living creature requires high welfare standards and simply cannot be put away like a fishing rod or a set of golf clubs. If it becomes ill for any reason, specialist avian veterinary surgeons must be consulted, which again, can be a very expensive proposition. What about holidays, did he know of anyone capable of properly caring for the bird in his absence?

My final words to him were to forget even thinking about getting a hawk at this stage, until he had spent a few months at least learning about the art of falconry and I hadn't even begun to explain the methods of training and the amount of time and patience required. When he was ready, and if he was still of a mind to practice falconry, I suggested he contact a reliable breeder who would supply him with the right hawk, together with any relevant and legal paperwork, such as an Article 10 certificate for any raptor found naturally in the United Kingdom and also that some species, such as the goshawk and golden eagle also required a registration document which would also show the ring numbers and origin of the parent birds, although the Harris hawk, I informed him would require no such documentation as it was not a species found in the wild in this country. I don't know for sure if he was pleased or not that he came to the falconry event, as his head was obviously spinning, but I suspect that it probably saved the life of a hawk had he continued without proper advice. I never saw, or heard anything from him afterwards, even though I gave him my contact details should he require any further information.

Budding Billy Casper fans should take careful note of the above.

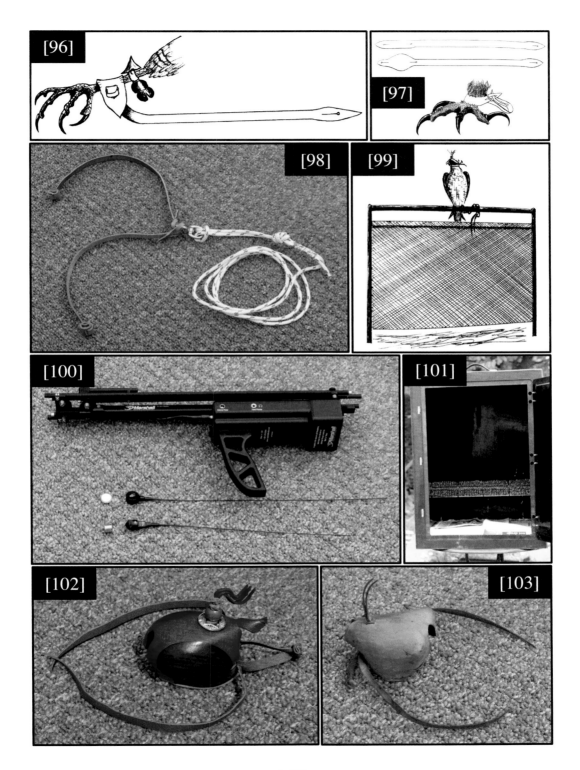

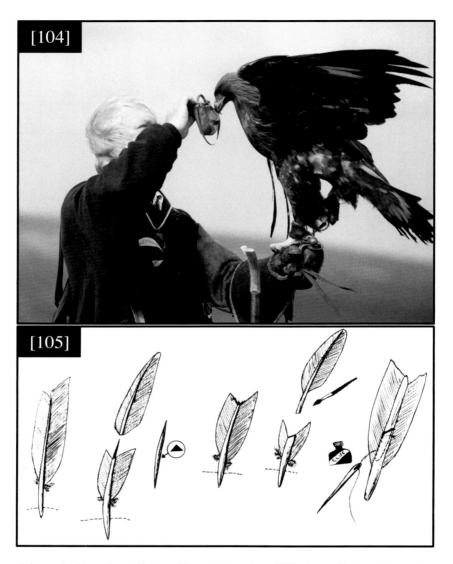

[96] Aylmeri jess, bell and traditional bewit *in situ*. [97] A traditional jess demonstrating the method of attachment. [98] A loop leash attached to a swivel and mews jesses. [99] A screen perch (as used in *Kes*), though today most raptors are free-lofted. [100] A Field Marshall digital radio telemetry system with Powermax and RT+ transmitters. More complex GPS systems are now available. [101] A travel box showing the interior. [102 & 103] A Dutch and Anglo Indian type hood respectively. These are used for keeping hawks calm, especially during the early stages of training. [104] The author using the hood on his male golden eagle, Star (Courtesy of Alex Hyde). [105] Methods of imping (replacing) broken flight and tail feathers i.e. using (left to right) traditional metal, or bamboo needle, or stitching.

Appendix 3

Location Maps

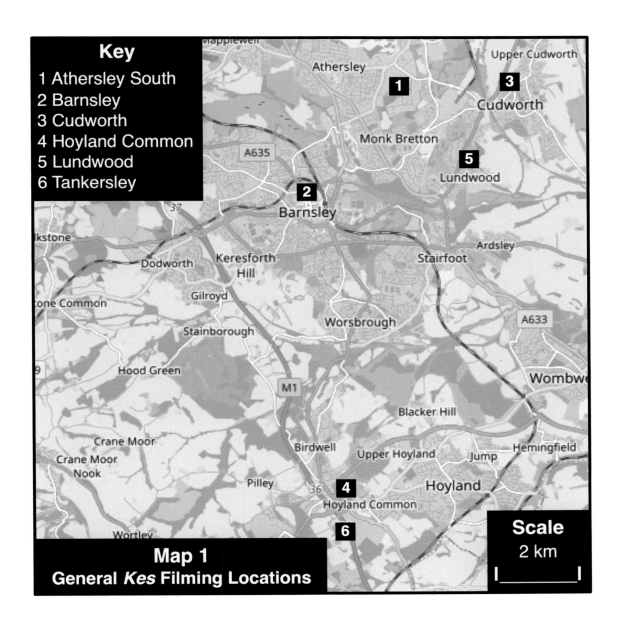

Key

1 Athersley South
2 Barnsley
3 Cudworth
4 Hoyland Common
5 Lundwood
6 Tankersley

Map 1
General *Kes* Filming Locations

Scale
2 km

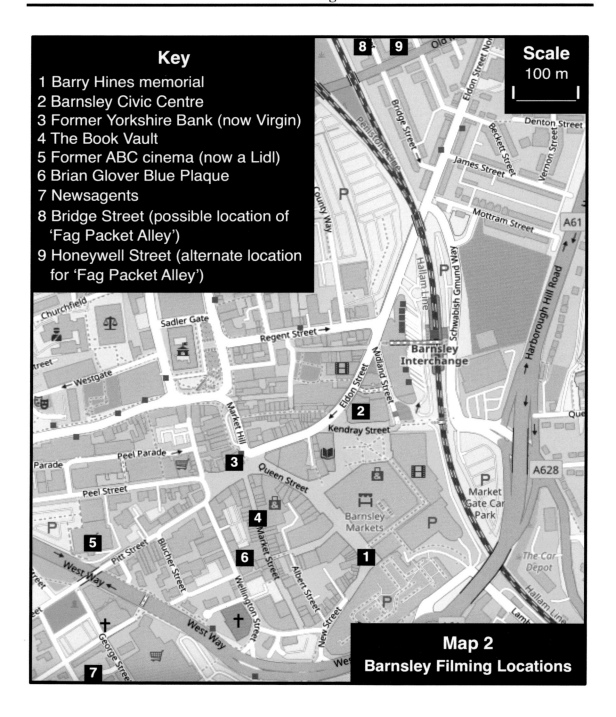

Key

1 Barry Hines memorial
2 Barnsley Civic Centre
3 Former Yorkshire Bank (now Virgin)
4 The Book Vault
5 Former ABC cinema (now a Lidl)
6 Brian Glover Blue Plaque
7 Newsagents
8 Bridge Street (possible location of 'Fag Packet Alley')
9 Honeywell Street (alternate location for 'Fag Packet Alley')

Map 2
Barnsley Filming Locations

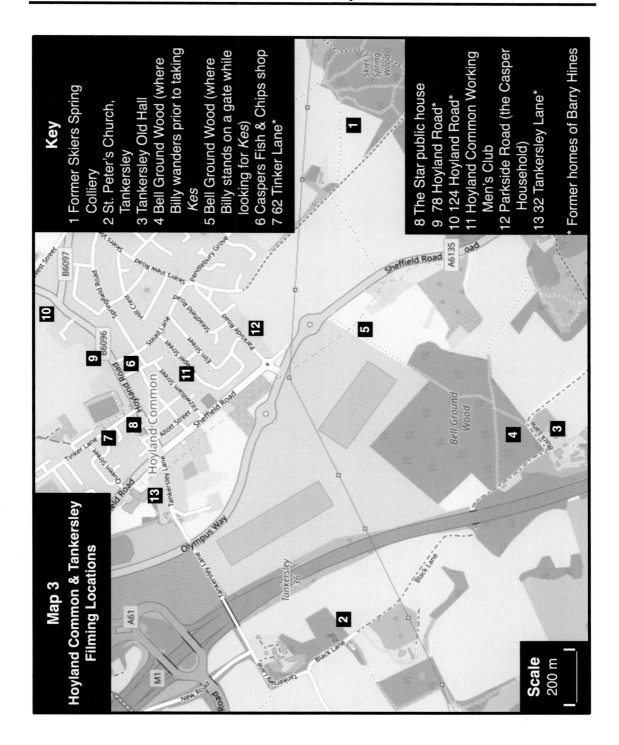

Key

1 Former Skiers Spring Colliery
2 St. Peter's Church, Tankersley
3 Tankersley Old Hall
4 Bell Ground Wood (where Billy wanders prior to taking *Kes*
5 Bell Ground Wood (where Billy stands on a gate while looking for *Kes*)
6 Caspers Fish & Chips shop
7 62 Tinker Lane*

8 The Star public house
9 78 Hoyland Road*
10 124 Hoyland Road*
11 Hoyland Common Working Men's Club
12 Parkside Road (the Casper Household)
13 32 Tankersley Lane*

* Former homes of Barry Hines

Map 3
Hoyland Common & Tankersley Filming Locations

Scale
200 m

Kes Locations as identified by What3Words.com

What3Words	Map	Location	Description
Scenes.Ending.Critic	1	1	Athersley South: Holy Trinity School (location of the football match)
Recall.Chef.Varieties	1	2	Barnsley: See Map 2 locations
Chair.Apart.Hobbies	1	3	Cudworth: Former site of the Cudworth Hotel
Impose.Walled.Shoulders	1	4	Hoyland Common: See Map 3 locations
Nature.Hope.Belong	1	5	Lundwood: Lewis Road (where Billy meets the milkman)
Banana.Speak.Fancy	1	5	Lundwood: Harrington Court (where the title credits were filmed)
Generated.Sulked.Copiers	1	6	Tankersley: See Map 3 locations
Lately.Bland.Lift	2	1	Barry Hines Memorial
Trail.Soap.Gazed.	2	2	Barnsley Civic Hall
Proper.Vase.Latter	2	3	Former Yorkshire Bank (now Virgin)
Retire.Dark.Deals	2	4	The Book Vault
River.Beats.Press	2	5	Former ABC cinema (now a Lidl)
Timing.Rash.Valley	2	6	Brian Glover Blue Plaque
Precautions.Recent.With	2	7	Newsagents
Nature.Flown.Backed	2	8	Bridge Street (possible location for 'Fag Packet Alley')
Urban.Wedge.Remote	2	9	Honeywell Street (alternate location for 'Fag packet Alley')
Nipping.Botanists.Guard	3	1	Former Skiers Spring Colliery

Sweeping.Intervals.Shame	3	2	St. Peter's Church, Tankersley
Erupted.Composts.Fermented	3	3	Tankersley Old Hall
Regular.Sheds.Unloaded	3	4	Bell Ground Wood (where Billy wanders prior to taking *Kes*)
Blotches.Swipes.Mole	3	5	Bell Ground Wood (where Billy stands on a gate while looking for *Kes*)
Snap.Travels.Radiates	3	6	Caspers Fish & Chips shop
Clef.Advice.Overt	3	7	62 Tinker Lane (former residence of Barry Hines)
Custodial.Changing.Burst	3	8	The Star public house
Exonerate.Marzipan.Bracelet	3	9	78 Hoyland Road (former residence of Barry Hines)
Mouth.Chill.Mats	3	10	124 Hoyland Road (former residence of Barry Hines)
Panting.Dispensed.Swells	3	11	Hoyland Common Working Men's Club
Confirms.Startles.Glows	3	12	Parkside Road (the Casper Household)
Coasting.Pulps.Embraced	3	13	32 Tankersley Lane (former residence of Barry Hines)

Appendix 4

Further *Kes* Related Reading

Forrest, David & Vice, Sue, *Barry Hines: Kes, Threads and beyond*, Manchester University Press, (2018), ISBN: 978-1-784992-62-0, 240 pages.

Golding, Simon W., *Life After Kes*, Apex Publishing Ltd., (2016), ISBN: 978-0-993337-15-4, 306 pages.

Hines, Barry, *A Kestrel for a Knave*, Penguin Classics, (2000), ISBN: 978-1-141184-98-2, 208 pages.

Hines, Richard, *No Way But Gentlenesse: A Memoir of How Kes, My Kestrel, Changed My Life*, Bloomsbury Publishing, (2016), ISBN: 978—408868-01-0, 288 pages.

Hines, Richard, *Kes to Fanshaw*, *The Falconer* (Journal of the British Falconers' Club), (2009), P140-147.

Steele, Ronnie, *Build it for Barry: Memoirs of a working-class northerner*, Arc Publishing & Print, (2021), ISBN 978-1-906722-85-2, 148 pages.

Steele, Ronnie, *A Blue Plaque for Brian Glover: True stories about growing up in the North*, Arc Publishing & Print, (2022), ISBN: 978-1-906722-91-3, 182 pages.

Wright, Chrissie, *A Kestrel for a Knave*, Barry Hines, Pearson Education, (1997), ISBN: 978-0-582314-02-3, 80 pages.

Acknowledgements

I would like to thank firstly, the late Barry Hines, who, without his amazing talent as a writer, *A Kestrel for a Knave*, and the film *Kes*, would never have become a reality. Also, to Barry's younger brother Richard, from whose experiences much of the book was based and for his permission to use the text of his filmed interview at the unveiling of the Kes statue in Hoyland library. Richard Hines also gave me some much-appreciated constructive criticism regarding my first draft of this manuscript, which I have applied. Without the foresight of the director, Ken Loach, and the producer, the late Tony Garnett, and the cinematographer, Chris Menges, the film almost certainly would never have reached our screens, or at least, not in the unique way that it was so expertly portrayed. Also, my gratitude to all the cast and crew who performed their duties to perfection, some of whom, in fact, most of the adult cast, have now sadly passed away.

I would also like to thank my son David for his help and companionship during our visits to Barnsley, Hoyland Common, Tankersley and Sheffield. Thanks also to Dave Rose, late of Caspers Fish & Chips shop in Hoyland Common, who not only provided us with excellent sustenance, but also provided information on some *Kes* filming locations and information regarding Greg Davies's *Looking for Kes* documentary. It was also Dave's suggestion that I write this book. I would also like to thank Professor David Forrest of Sheffield University for all his help whilst visiting the Barry Hines Archives in the Special Collections Department and for his signing my copy of his book, *Barry Hines Kes, Threads and Beyond*. I would also like to thank Laura Smith-Brown, Special Collections Manager, and Eleanor Mulkeen-Parker, Special Collections Heritage and Archive Assistant at the Western Bank Library, Sheffield University for all their help with my photography within the Barry Hines Archive. My heartfelt thanks go to Ronnie Steele and the Kes Group and the Bringing Kes Home Group. I am deeply indebted for Ronnie's unflinching help and his support in providing me with much information and photographs which would have been very difficult to obtain elsewhere. Through the good offices of Ronnie Steele, I would like to thank Barry Hines's first wife, Margaret Hines, for permission to use the 1968 photograph of David 'Dai' Bradley and Barry Hines with two of the Kestrels that were used in the making of *Kes* and several other *Kes* related images. Also, through Ronnie Steele, I would also like to thank artist Richard Kitson for the use of his excellent painting of Billy Casper and the famous two-fingered salute **[See Front Cover]**. Ronnie put me straight on several issues for which I am truly grateful, and his help was invaluable. My thanks go to Faye Steel, Sonja Walker, and Tony the caretaker for arranging for me to take photographs from the roof of the Holy Trinity School at Athersley South, Barnsley, of the famous football field, and other areas of the school. And last but certainly not least to the many people of Barnsley and Hoyland Common who we met on our travels, from market traders to people shopping in the streets, all of whom were so friendly and helpful, I heartily thank you all.